A Teacher's Guide to
COOPERATIVE DISCIPLINE

How to Manage Your Classroom and Promote Self-Esteem

Linda Albert, Ph.D.

Will Roy, Ph.D., and Andy LePage, Ph.D.
Contributing Authors

this product
is distributed in
Canada by

PSYCAN

P.O. Box 290, Station V
Toronto, Ontario
M6R 3A5
1-800-263-3558

1796

AGS® staff participating in the development and production of this publication:

Project Team

Marjorie Lisovskis, Managing Editor
Julie Nauman, Designer
Mary Kaye Kuzma, Production Coordinator
Steven Moravetz, Marketing Associate

Product Development

Dorothy Chapman, Director of Instructional Materials
Lynne Cromwell, Publishing Services Manager
Bonnie Goldsmith, Acquisitions Editor
Charles Pederson, Copy Editor
Maureen Wilson, Art Director

Project Editor

Judith Wardwell O'Donnell

Cartoons

John Bush

Cover Design

Terry Dugan, Terry Dugan Design

To my son, Steven Moraff,
with much love and appreciation
for the richness you bring to my life

Other works by the author

Coping with Kids

Coping with Kids and School

Coping with Kids and Vacation

Quality Parenting
(with Michael Popkin)

Stepfamily Living Series
(with Elizabeth Einstein)

Strengthening Your Stepfamily
(with Elizabeth Einstein)

Contents

Preface

I wrote this book because I am an idealist. I believe students will cooperate in the classroom if given the chance. I believe teachers will use positive discipline techniques to give them that chance. I believe parents will support our efforts in the classroom when they are respectfully invited to join us as true partners in the educational process.

I'm also a realist. I know that disorder in the classroom is a major threat to a student's education and a teacher's sanity. That's why I've spent so many years of my life developing *Cooperative Discipline*. Its purpose is to show educators and students how to change this reality and develop schools and classrooms where students enjoy learning and where teachers look forward to going to work each day.

The development of *Cooperative Discipline* was certainly a cooperative effort! The process involved folks of all ages who gave generously of their insight and expertise:

My students were some of my best teachers. Through their behavior, they taught me which discipline strategies worked and which failed. With their smiles, their cooperation, and their eagerness to learn, they encouraged me when I was on the right track. I wish there were some way to thank each of these young people personally.

The teachers who enrolled in my graduate courses and inservice workshops contributed many of the strategies and techniques described in these pages. Through the years I have kept cumulative lists of their many wonderful ideas—generated during sharing and brainstorming sessions—which were then refined, organized, and field-tested for inclusion in this book. I send a heartfelt thank-you to all of these creative individuals.

It is no accident that my teacher workshops were called "Maintaining Sanity in the Classroom," for this is the title of the required text, written by Rudolf Dreikurs, Floy Pepper, and Bernice Bronia Grunwald. A whole school of psychology has developed around the ideas of Dreikurs and his teacher, Alfred Adler; this is the theoretical basis of *Cooperative Discipline*. I want to thank my first teachers of Adlerian psychology—Oscar Christensen, Bill Marchant, and Bill Hillman—for introducing me to these concepts.

Many wonderful people gave freely of their time to serve on the *Cooperative Discipline* Advisory Board, reading the various drafts of the manuscript and offering constructive feedback. These folks I thank personally: Nancy Berla, Betty Lou Bettner, Lynn Bounds, Mary Bullerman, Betty Castor, Don Darling, Stan Dubelle, Ray Huntington, Patricia Kyle, Amy Lew, John Lizer, John Lucas, Al Mance, Cameron Meredith, Sue Mihalik, Edna Nash, Robert Reasoner, Sharon Robinson, and Barbara and Robert Turk.

A second advisory board was composed of teenagers. After all, who knows better what works with students than the students themselves? These young adults, who took the time to read the manuscript and discuss the ideas with me, are all members of the JCPenney Teen S.T.A.F.F. program located in the Tampa Bay area. To each of these teens, and to Susan Wendt—the very talented originator and director of the program—my sincere thanks.

Dozens of people took part in the field testing of *Cooperative Discipline*. They attended inservice sessions and then tried out the ideas in their classrooms, subsequently giving written feedback that was most helpful in revising the original draft to this final form. A hearty thanks to each of you.

As I developed *Cooperative Discipline,* I learned that the task of transforming a teaching outline into a book is not an easy one. Without the help of editors, I would have drowned in a sea of words. Three editors pored over this manuscript. First there was Judith Rachel, who took the raw words and made them readable. Next came Lois Welshons, who helped make all the ideas flow in an organized manner. Last, but by no means least, Judy O'Donnell joined the team and added her precision with words and phrases, which gave the manuscript a final polish. My deepest thanks go to each of you for your expertise, wisdom, and patience.

Anyone who lives with a writer has to be a little crazy. Writers wail when words are blocked. They throw temper tantrums when deadlines approach too soon. They worry over each new draft, certain that they have inadvertently omitted some idea of monumental importance. Through all of these travails my husband, Byron Eakin, has stood by me: encouraging me when I was down, pushing me when I was stuck, and bolstering my confidence when I ceased to believe that I could ever finish these pages. Thank you, Byron, for being my guiding light. I promise to give you a breather before I start the next book. Even crazy people have limits.

Linda Albert
October, 1989

1

SECTION ONE

Cooperative Discipline: Theory and Practice

Young people choose different behaviors to feel significant and important in different groups—the family, the class, the Scout troop, the drama club, the ball team. When we recognize this need to belong, we're on our way to helping students choose appropriate behavior to achieve their special place in our classroom.

CHAPTER 1

The Program: Practical and Positive

All teachers—elementary or secondary, new or experienced—face discipline challenges. Beginning with our first day on the job, we steadily learn that students have hundreds of ways to annoy us and their classmates and to disrupt our teaching. For example, consider the behavior of two fictitious, but not atypical, students:

> *Fourth-grader Dexter Darius consistently fails to turn in his homework. At least once a day, he refuses to take out a book when asked to do so. When his teacher insists that he produce the book, Dexter responds by slamming the book down on his desk. While standing in line for lunch or recess, Dexter frequently shoves or pokes classmates. When corrected for such behavior, Dexter denies doing it and mutters threats under his breath.*
>
> ————
>
> *Dana Darling, a high school sophomore, regularly comes late to history class. She usually fails to bring her notebook to class, and when the teacher asks her to get it, Dana responds, "You can't make me!" Dana never participates voluntarily in class discussions and refuses to respond when she's called on directly.*

A safe generalization is that we've all encountered clones of Dexter or Dana in our classrooms. How we respond to their behavior depends on our philosophy of discipline, which can be grouped into one of three general approaches:

- Educators subscribing to a "hands-off" approach believe that young people develop their behavior based on internal controls and that they eventually learn to make the right decisions. These teachers assume the role of a bystander who, at most, helps a student clarify what is happening. A discipline program that emphasizes only communication skills is based on the hands-off approach.

- Educators using a "hands-on" approach believe that external controls are needed for the proper development of youngsters. These teachers assume the role of a boss, taking charge by demanding, commanding, and directing. A discipline program that involves behavior modification and assertive techniques is based on the hands-on approach.

- Educators employing a "hands-joined" approach believe that young people's behavior is the product of both internal and external forces. These teachers assume the role of a cooperative leader, guiding students by offering choices, setting limits, and involving students in the process. A discipline program that builds positive relationships as well as self-esteem through encouragement techniques is based on the hands-joined approach.

Cooperative Discipline, as a practical and positive program, takes the hands-joined approach to dealing with misbehavior. To put it simply, *Cooperative Discipline* shows teachers how to work hand-in-hand with students, colleagues, and parents. With *cooperative* as the byword, two achievements are possible: first, a classroom becomes a pleasant place in which to teach and learn, and, second, students gain self-esteem, a prerequisite for good behavior as well as for academic achievement.

Too good to be true? Not if we accept the premise of the *Cooperative Discipline* process—that we, as teachers, have enormous power in influencing our students' behavior.

The Key: Quality of Teacher-Student Interaction

Determining exactly what students expect from us and what we expect from students is the key to creating positive classroom behavior. Teacher-student interaction is a two-way street: the students relate to us, and we relate to the students. When students choose to relate to us through misbehavior, we have to be able to recognize the purpose, or the *goal,* of the misbehavior and know how to respond to it both immediately and in the long term.

Cooperative Discipline provides teachers with the skills necessary to identify the goal of a particular misbehavior and with specific intervention techniques that can be used at the moment of the misbehavior. But the program also looks beyond the teacher-student interaction brought about by the misbehavior, suggesting practical ways of creating future positive interactions that build student self-esteem.

Cooperative Discipline offers a process that's both corrective and supportive. Most of us would acknowledge that reliance on intervention techniques alone to stop misbehavior provides only temporary relief; we can depend on a recurrence of the misbehavior. On the other hand, if we couple intervention with steps for building self-esteem, we'll usually achieve positive relationships with our students and, consequently, appropriate behavior that lasts.

The Goal: Cooperative Relationships In and Beyond the Classroom

The *Cooperative Discipline* process not only encourages a positive relationship between teacher and student but also between teacher and parent, teacher and teacher, and teacher and administrator. Achieving such cooperation is not an easy task, since parents, students, teachers, and administrators often play the "blame game" when misbehavior is the issue. They tend to point the finger at one another or at contemporary influences such as popular song lyrics and movie themes or at societal problems such as unemployment, child abuse, and drug abuse. The blame game has no winner; every player's token remains stuck on the problem, rather than moving forward to achieve active solutions.

Educators, parents, and students play the blame game for a variety of reasons. Perhaps they feel powerless in the face of what seems to be an overwhelming problem. Perhaps they believe they can't control detrimental influences in the modern world. Perhaps they don't think they personally can make a difference. Perhaps they don't want to admit that they don't know what to do next.

Cooperative Discipline suggests alternatives to the blame game by showing concretely how parents, students, and educators can work together to solve discipline dilemmas. The program provides specific suggestions on how to establish a workable partnership that can make a difference in behavior no matter what environmental factors are at work.

The "blame game" has no winners.

The Framework: Time-Tested and Practical

Cooperative Discipline represents a synthesis of theories about behavior and discipline translated into practical skills and strategies. The theories are up-to-date, respected ideas about human development, communication, and cooperation. Since young people reflect the values and behaviors that they see around them, they must be approached with modern methods for effective discipline.

Forming the theoretical framework of the program are the philosophy and psychology of Alfred Adler and Rudolf Dreikurs as well as compatible theories of William Glasser, Albert Ellis, and Eric Berne. Their ideas have been tested and refined by thousands of educators and are used successfully by many other professionals, from therapists to business consultants, to help people live and work together harmoniously.

Cooperative Discipline is also based on my own experiences as a classroom teacher and on ideas I've exchanged with teachers throughout the country while presenting workshops dealing with the discipline techniques of Dreikurs. The program has been refined on the basis of field-test comments from teachers and administrators in twenty school districts as well as with the aid of two advisory boards, one composed of educators and the other of teenagers.

The Action Plan: Theories Become Practice

No discipline program can be effective unless its theories can be put into practice. Within the *Cooperative Discipline* process, theories are translated into a useful diagnostic, corrective, and prescriptive tool—the School Action Plan. The plan enables teachers to develop discipline strategies specific to an individual student's needs through the completion of five action steps:

1. Pinpoint and describe the student's behavior.
2. Identify the goal of the misbehavior.
3. Choose intervention techniques for the moment of misbehavior.
4. Select encouragement techniques to build self-esteem.
5. Involve parents as partners.

A School Action Plan helps teachers determine how to interact with a particular student. We actually write the plan to guide our behavior toward a student; that is, so we can respond to the student's misbehavior with reasoned effort rather than reacting in a reflexive manner.

We don't need to develop a School Action Plan by ourselves. At any step in the process, we might ask for assistance from other teachers, administrators, and support-service personnel. Why go it alone when we're surrounded by colleagues whose advice and encouragement can make all the difference in the world?

Besides providing a definite course for dealing with misbehavior, the School Action Plan can be an invaluable aid in conferences with students, parents, and other school personnel. The plan not only clarifies concerns about misbehavior but also provides a format for discussion. If parents want to model the School Action Plan for use at home, they can be assisted in preparing a Home Action Plan.

The Winner: The Entire School Community

The entire school community wins when *Cooperative Discipline* is implemented. Immediate winners are the teachers. They gain the knowledge and skills to cope with classroom behaviors that previously drove them to distraction. As their daily discipline struggles decrease, their satisfaction in teaching increases. As they learn how to build and strengthen quality relationships with their students, they feel better not only about the students but also about themselves. The possibility of teacher burnout, a real hazard of everyday classroom life, is reduced.

The *Cooperative Discipline* approach is useful for teachers of all levels, from kindergarten through high school. The basics of behavior and the dynamics of teacher-student interactions remain constant no matter what age the student.

What *does* change according to student age is the applicability of intervention and encouragement techniques. Therefore, *Cooperative Discipline* includes a variety of techniques appropriate for various age groups.

Students also are winners in the *Cooperative Discipline* process. My experience tells me that students are almost as upset as the teacher when misbehavior disrupts a class. Students want to learn in an orderly, firm-yet-friendly classroom atmosphere. When they have that opportunity, their academic performance is likely to rise. Moreover, their self-esteem is nurtured as their teacher employs the encouragement strategies that are basic to *Cooperative Discipline*.

Parents benefit from the *Cooperative Discipline* process too. They gain confidence and optimism from knowing that their child's school behavior is being guided according to a specific, carefully constructed plan of action. Many parents also welcome the opportunity to participate in the *Cooperative Discipline* process by developing and carrying out a Home Action Plan that parallels the School Action Plan.

Finally, administrators are winners because *Cooperative Discipline* can be modeled with consistency throughout a school. In addition, a written Action Plan serves as an accountability tool that allows an administrator to quickly review and evaluate a teacher's course for working with a difficult student. And, perhaps even more important, it allows the administrator to know when it's necessary to offer assistance.

Getting Started: The Process Unfolds

The chapters that follow explain the *Cooperative Discipline* process, both the theories and the practice. Working through the chapters consecutively is recommended since they often build on one another. Skipping the Chapter 2 discussion about behavior concepts may be tempting, but an understanding of these concepts is intrinsic to following the process effectively. When the theory has been digested, we can begin the practical process, which involves taking objective, corrective, supportive, and cooperative action as we develop a School Action Plan. As the *Cooperative Discipline* process unfolds, these are the major topics that will be explored:

- what students are trying to achieve when they misbehave
- how to devise specific School Action Plans for misbehaving students
- intervention techniques to use at the moment of misbehavior
- how to reinforce desirable behavior
- how to build self-esteem using encouragement techniques
- how to discipline cooperatively

One last word. *Cooperative Discipline* isn't a magic panacea that will solve all classroom discipline problems instantly. Rather, it's a process to follow over time for constructing creative, positive, and personalized solutions to discipline problems. Moreover, as you implement the ideas presented, you'll recognize that you're the actual educational model of *Cooperative Discipline*. The success of the program depends on you and the dynamics of your powerful influence on your students' lives.

CHAPTER 2

The Framework: Concepts of Behavior

Whether you're a new or experienced teacher, whether you work with elementary, middle school, or high school students, you've probably wrestled with certain questions about student behavior over and over again: How can I convince misbehaving students to stop what they're doing? How can I inspire well-behaved students to continue to cooperate? How can I motivate passive students to respond? The answers to these questions begin with an understanding of the three basic concepts of behavior:

1. Students choose their behavior.
2. The ultimate goal of student behavior is to fulfill the need to belong.
3. Students misbehave to achieve one of four immediate goals.

Concept 1: *Students choose their behavior.*

Troy is tardy for English class daily and always hands in assignments late. Why? Shawn is always willing to do work for extra credit. Why? Joyce mutters four-letter words under her breath during geometry class. Why? Sumiko is always the first to volunteer to stay after school to help with classroom tasks. Why?

The answer is simple: Because they choose to behave in this way.

Many psychologists suggest far more complex explanations of behavior: that it is based on childhood experiences, or on instinctive needs, heredity, environment, or conditioned responses. Such insights, however true or false they may be, do not help us maintain discipline in the classroom. For example, Troy's teacher can't do anything to change Troy's early childhood experiences, and Joyce's teacher can't change the DNA of Joyce's cells. Shawn's enthusiasm for extra credit may be prompted by his parents' promise of a dollar for every A on his report card. His teacher can't easily change the parents' means of motivation. Sumiko's impulse to help may be the result of her reluctance to go home to an unhappy situation. Her teacher can't change Sumiko's home life.

As teachers, we can't go back into a student's past to right a wrong, nor can we change a student's life outside of school. Understanding that behavior is based on choice, however, can provide us with strategic leverage in coping with the inappropriate behavior of the Troys and Joyces and in encouraging the positive behavior of the Shawns and Sumikos.

The proof that Joyce chooses her behavior is that she behaves differently in different situations. In her 8:00 A.M. English class, Joyce pays attention and contributes to discussions. Mrs. Hernandez, the English teacher, describes Joyce as a "bright, cooperative, alert youngster who relates well to her peers." An hour later, in Mr. McCracken's geometry class, Joyce mutters obscene words, talks out of turn, and refuses to complete assignments. Mr. McCracken describes Joyce as a "nuisance who disrupts my teaching and distracts other students."

Does Joyce's family environment change between eight and nine o'clock? Do her genes shift? Of course not. In both classes, Joyce chooses behavior that makes sense to her.

Do rules make students choose positive behavior? How we wish that were the case! Almost all students know both the classroom and school rules and, if asked, could recite them forward and backward. When six-year-old Teddy runs in the hall, has he forgotten the rule about walking in the hall? When fifteen-year-old Tess saunters into class five minutes after the last bell, has she forgotten the rule about coming to class on time? No. Teddy and Tess have *chosen* to "forget" the rules. Teddy's teacher can tell him to stop running in the hall until she's blue in the face, but Teddy won't stop running until *he chooses* to walk. The decision to change is Teddy's alone; the rule exists, but neither the rule nor the teacher's repetition of it can make Teddy choose to obey it.

No one and no situation can make anyone behave in a certain way. Though people and events and conditioning may invite a particular behavior, the invitation can be accepted or rejected. The choice exists. Once we understand that behavior is based on choice, we can begin to influence a student's decisions about how to behave. The change starts with us: we need to learn how to interact with students so they will want to choose appropriate behavior and comply with the rules.

YOU CAN'T REALLY BLAME ME FOR CAUSING TROUBLE, MS. MARGOLE... IT'S A GENETIC PREDISPOSITION.

Reminding ourselves that behavior is based on choice can give us some strategic leverage.

Concept 2: The ultimate goal of student behavior is to fulfill the need to belong.

The need to belong, which means "to feel significant and important," is basic. People live in social groupings—the home, the school, the workplace—and can't survive without one another. Since students spend at least six hours a day in school, their ability to find a satisfying place in the classroom group is of major importance.

To experience a strong sense of belonging in school, students must satisfy the "three Cs."[1] They need to feel *capable* of completing tasks in a manner that meets the standards of the school. They need to believe they can *connect* successfully with teachers and classmates. They need to know they *contribute* in a significant way to the group.

Students seek to satisfy the three Cs in the way that makes the most sense to them at the time. When they believe they are unable to be capable, to connect, or to contribute by behaving appropriately, they may try to achieve their goal of belonging by misbehaving. Three factors affect students' ability to satisfy the three Cs in the classroom:

- the quality of the teacher-student relationship
- the strength of the classroom climate for success
- the appropriateness of the classroom structure[2]

With these factors in mind, consider again the divergent behaviors of Joyce in Mrs. Hernandez's first-period English class and in Mr. McCracken's second-period geometry class. A fair assumption would be that Joyce behaves appropriately in English because she and Mrs. Hernandez have a positive relationship based on mutual respect (Joyce *connects*), because she experiences a sense of success in her English classwork (she feels *capable*), and because she can learn and exchange ideas within the classroom structure that's been established (she *contributes*). In contrast, Joyce is unable to satisfy the three Cs positively in geometry class, so she chooses to satisfy some through misbehavior. She connects with Mr. McCracken in an uncooperative manner, but nonetheless forces him to relate to her. She satisfies her need to feel capable by refusing to do assignments; after all, if she did them and failed, she would feel incapable. Unfortunately, the structure of the class prevents Joyce from taking the opportunity to contribute in any significant way.

Joyce's Jekyll-and-Hyde behavior is not atypical. Most of us have witnessed students with such dual behaviors, and we've also observed students who consistently behave or misbehave. In the same classroom, we have students who continually choose to work and learn with us, and we have students who choose not to work and learn, no matter how hard we try to involve them. The students who misbehave have the same ultimate goal as the students who behave—to fulfill their need to belong by being able to satisfy the three Cs. Once we become aware of this need, we can help the satisfied students continue to feel satisfied, and we can help the dissatisfied find ways to achieve satisfaction.

The need to belong also explains why some young people exhibit behavior at school that's markedly different from their behavior at home. For example, some of us may have experienced a conversation similar to this:

Teacher: Egbert's been a feisty terror for the past month. Not a day goes by without him picking a fight. He got a black eye today because he called the captain of the football team a "wimp."

Mr. Eager: Egbert? Why, I don't understand. He's always the perfect gentleman at home!

That Mr. Eager is turning a blind eye at home is possible; however, that he's honestly reporting Egbert's behavior is equally possible. The same young man who is driving his teacher to distraction may not act up at home. Egbert may have found acceptable ways to connect, feel capable, and contribute at home. In school, Egbert hasn't found an appropriate way to satisfy his need to belong.

This parent-teacher scenario may also seem familiar:

Teacher: I want to compliment you, Mrs. Schultz. Angelica is one of the most courteous and cooperative children I've ever taught.

Mrs. Schultz: You must have the wrong folder on your desk! My daughter is a little monster who drives everyone batty at home. You must be talking about someone else's child.

Angelica clearly has found positive ways to live up to her name at school, but she has been unable to discover how to feel capable, how to connect, and how to contribute at home. Consequently, parent and teacher are experiencing contrasting behaviors from the same child.

Young people choose different behaviors to feel significant and important in different groups—the family, the class, the Scout troop, the drama club, the ball team. When we recognize this need to belong, we're on our way to helping students choose appropriate behavior to achieve their special place in our classroom.

Concept 3: Students misbehave to achieve one of four immediate goals.

When students choose misbehavior over positive behavior, what do they hope to gain? Ultimately, they're seeking their place in the group (Concept 2). Along the way, however, they've become frustrated in trying to achieve the three Cs in a positive manner, so they misbehave in an attempt to obtain immediate gratification. What they want usually corresponds to one of these four goals:

Attention. Some students choose misbehavior to get extra attention. They want to be center stage all the time, and constantly distract the teacher and classmates to gain an audience.

Power. Some students misbehave in a quest for power. They want to be the boss—of themselves, of the teacher, sometimes even of the whole class. At the very least, they want to show others that "you can't push me around." They refuse to comply with classroom rules or teacher requests, and often disrupt the established order.

When children are unable to connect by behaving positively,
they resort to misbehavior to achieve their goal.

Revenge. Some students want to lash out to get even for real or imagined hurts. The target of the revenge may be the teacher, other students, or both.

Avoidance-of-failure. Some students want to avoid repeated failure. They believe they can't live up to their own, their teacher's, or their parents' expectations. To compensate for this feeling of failure, they choose withdrawal behaviors that make them appear inadequate or disabled. Their hope is that everyone will back off and leave them alone so they won't have to be reminded that they aren't making the grade.

These four goals of misbehavior were first postulated in the 1930s by the noted educator Dr. Rudolf Dreikurs. When Dreikurs was asked why he had determined four goals instead of three, five, or eight, he reportedly responded, "I didn't make up these categories. I went out and observed children, and this is what I found."

If we carefully observe a student's misbehavior, we'll usually be able to identify its immediate goal as attention, power, revenge, or avoidance-of-failure. Admittedly, this sounds simplistic. Does every misbehavior really have one of these four goals? Of course not. No theory, no matter how complete, applies to every situation 100 percent of the time. In my years of teaching, however, knowledge of the four goals has helped me classify about 90 percent of student misbehaviors. That's not a bad percentage, so until something better comes along, I'll stick with Dreikurs's theory.

Whether a student misbehaves for attention, power, revenge, or to avoid failure, we're forced into responding; we have to interact with the student. If we're able to identify the goal of the misbehavior, we can interact capably not only at once but also over time. Right away, we can redirect the misbehavior by using an intervention technique that suits the misbehavior. Over time, we can work toward eliminating further occurrences of the misbehavior by using encouragement techniques that build self-esteem. With time, the student will learn appropriate ways to feel capable, to connect, and to contribute. Thus, a little knowledge can give us a lot of advantage.

In our interactions with misbehaving students, we need to keep in mind that we can only *influence* their behavior. We can't change their behavior, for only *they* have this power of choice (Concept 1). But influencing such change becomes possible when we recognize that misbehavior is usually directed toward one of the four goals. The goals become our major clues in solving the misbehavior mystery. Once we're wise to what students are hoping to gain through misbehavior, we can help them find legitimate ways to satisfy their need to belong, ways that take their personal point of view into account. Consequently, we'll be on our way to creating a classroom environment that encourages appropriate behavior, fosters self-esteem, and motivates achievement.

Putting the Concepts into Action

Can we really influence students to abandon annoying and disruptive behaviors and to choose positive behaviors instead? We can—if we use the vantage point provided by the three basic concepts of behavior. I can cite my own classroom experience as an example. Before understanding these concepts, I never tailored discipline strategies to the goals of misbehaviors or to my students' need to belong. Consequently, I was often frustrated because I couldn't "make" students behave.

Consider my relationship with a former fifth-grade student, Joey. Joey must have lain awake nights thinking of new ways to get under my skin. Every morning I wondered what torment he had in store for me that day. He seemed to have 101 misbehaviors and the ability to sabotage every discipline technique I tried. I was never prepared for what he did next—until I was introduced to the concepts of behavior.

Armed with the knowledge that behavior is based on choice, I was able to erase much frustrating and exhausting self-blame for failing to make Joey change his ways. I stopped trying to *make* Joey behave and switched to using techniques designed to convince him that he'd be better off *choosing* to behave.

Knowledge of the need to belong led me to make a greater effort to nurture my relationship with Joey. My attempts to discipline him no longer stopped at the intervention stage. Recognizing that Joey's misbehavior was a mistaken attempt to satisfy the three Cs, I began using specific encouragement techniques to influence him to choose positive ways to connect, feel capable, and contribute.

Likewise, knowing the four goals of misbehavior put me one step ahead of Joey, rather than twenty paces behind. Trying to make sense of Joey's 101 seemingly different misbehaviors had my head spinning, until I stopped viewing each incident of misbehavior as an isolated event. Instead, I learned to quickly categorize Joey's misbehavior according to its goal and then immediately apply an intervention that matched the goal.

Knowledge of the concepts of behavior changed the course of Joey's and my interactions. Our relationship wasn't transformed over one week or even two. But, gradually, mutual respect and, believe it or not, a bit of mutual liking blossomed between us. My experience with Joey exemplifies what has become the

Cooperative Discipline process. The process is sound because it's based on respected concepts about behavior. The process is workable because it translates the concepts into practical actions. And the process is cooperative because it recognizes that interactions must go beyond interventions if positive behavior is to become the choice.

The Truth Is in the Outcome

When I present workshops on *Cooperative Discipline,* teachers universally speculate on the veracity of the three basic concepts of behavior: "How do you know these concepts are true? You haven't provided scientific proof for them!"

My response is always the confession that no scientific proof justifies these principles. Theories about behavior are just that—theories. None are based on irrefutable scientific evidence. No one really knows the final and absolute truth about behavior.

Before you dismiss the concepts and this book, follow this suggestion and do what I do: Pretend that the concepts are true. Pretend that your students choose their behavior, that their ultimate need is to belong, that the goal of misbehavior can be categorized as attention, power, revenge, or avoidance-of-failure. If you adopt this attitude, I predict that you will experience positive changes in your classroom. Students who set your teeth on edge may become smiling and pleasant. Those who haven't done an honest day's work since September may become at least mildly enthusiastic about learning. Once you experience such changes, it won't matter whether the concepts are 100 percent true.

I've used these concepts of behavior in dealing with many students and with my own three children. Over the years, I've determined that they are the most effective ideas around. Until I'm convinced that other theories are more effective, I'll continue to believe in these concepts, and I invite you to do the same.

Notes

1. The three Cs are adapted from a concept developed by two psychotherapist-educators, Amy Lew and Betty Lou Bettner.
2. Linda Albert, *Coping with Kids and School* (New York: Dutton, 1984), 115.

CHAPTER 3

The Practical Process Begins: The School Action Plan

There's no one solution to all children's behavior problems. For example, consider this disciplinary guideline from a school handbook: "When a student knowingly breaks a school rule or endangers the safety of others, the student may be assigned to write a page out of the dictionary." Will copying page 636 of *Webster's* convince Nathan that it's wrong to bully younger children on the playground? Will writing out all the words and definitions from *peg* to *pen* influence Sabrina to get to her homeroom on time? Of course not. Discipline has to fit the misbehavior. Just as each student chooses a different set of behaviors based on a unique combination of causes and purposes, so must a school discipline program offer a variety of guidelines to plan unique solutions tailored to specific behavior problems.

Cooperative Discipline not only offers the needed variety of guidelines but also provides a practical planning tool for individualizing and applying these guidelines: the five-step School Action Plan. A sample School Action Plan can be found in Appendix E. A completed plan is a model for change. We write a plan to guide our interactions with a student, with the goal being to influence change in the student's behavior. The plan represents our commitment to encouraging the student to make appropriate choices while trying to satisfy that ultimate need—to belong.

Designing a School Action Plan takes time, but a thoughtfully composed plan has payoffs that reward our efforts. Just the act of planning can relieve our stress and frustration. As we write about a student's misbehavior and plot a course of action, we usually come to the realization that effecting change is possible. Transferring our observations and thoughts from mind to paper gives us a positive charge mentally; it removes uncertainty from the discipline process and replaces it with expectation for success.

Five Steps to Reasoned Effort

The process of designing a School Action Plan helps us view a student's misbehavior objectively so that we can determine the goal of the misbehavior, choose appropriate interventions, and select encouragement techniques. A School Action Plan thus becomes a diagnostic, corrective, and prescriptive tool that can guide us in devising a thoughtful response to a student's misbehavior, rather than reacting in an impulsive manner. All five steps of the School Action Plan are equally important, with each step building on the information we've gathered in the previous step. A completed plan is not only an individualized discipline program but also a process for guiding our interactions with a student. These are summaries of the action steps followed in preparing a School Action Plan:

Step 1: Pinpoint and Describe the Student's Behavior

Before we can help a student choose to stop misbehaving, we have to pinpoint and describe the behaviors that are causing us the most concern. We want to list only the three or four most troublesome behaviors, not every transgression the student has ever committed! Limiting this list may be frustrating when a student seems to have 537 miserable behaviors. Take heart. Each time we successfully redirect one behavior, we are chipping away at the student's perception that similar behaviors will satisfy his or her need to belong. By influencing a student's choices of how to satisfy this need, we'll be nurturing change in the student's overall behavior pattern, not just in the specific behaviors we've listed.

A student's troublesome behaviors need to be stated as objectively as possible. For instance, a description of George's behavior as "constantly disruptive" is too general and judgmental. Instead, what George does to disrupt the class has to be pinpointed. George may slam books on his desk, shout out answers without raising his hand, and hum to himself. These are the specific behaviors that are listed under Step 1 of the plan. The frequency and specific times of George's behaviors are also noted. "Constantly" is a subjective term and probably an exaggeration. George may shout out an average of five answers during math class only. He may hum only while working on compositions during English class.

To be effective, the intervention strategy needs to fit the misbehavior.

To obtain such accurate descriptions of a student's behaviors, we have to become accurate observers. One way to check the objectivity of our descriptions is to consider whether they could be documented by a video camera or tape recorder. If they could, then we can be satisfied that we've described the behaviors accurately.

Guidelines for objectively describing student behaviors are presented in Chapter 4 of this handbook.

Step 2: Identify the Goal of the Misbehavior

Once we've written objective descriptions of the behaviors causing concern, we have the necessary information to begin determining the immediate goal of the misbehavior. As discussed in Chapter 2, the goal is usually one of these four:

- attention
- power
- revenge
- avoidance-of-failure

Knowledge of the goal enables us to tailor intervention and encouragement techniques to the misbehavior. For example, if Sari is mouthing off to get attention, the teacher might move next to Sari's desk while continuing with the lesson at hand. Sari gets a minimal amount of attention, probably just enough to quiet her down. If Sari's goal is power, however, the teacher's nearby presence won't convince Sari to quiet down. Only when we recognize the goal of the misbehavior can we begin to interact effectively with a student.

Clues that help us identify the goal of a student's misbehavior concern first our response to the misbehavior, and then the student's response to our attempts to change the behavior. These clues are explained in each chapter relating to a particular goal (Chapters 5, 7, 8, 12).

Step 3: Choose Intervention Techniques for the Moment of Misbehavior

Steps 1 and 2 provide us with the necessary diagnostic information for completing this corrective step of the School Action Plan. While choosing intervention techniques, keep in mind that intervention does not mean punishment. Instead, think of intervention as guidance with a double purpose: to stop the behavior occurring at the moment and to influence the student to choose more appropriate behavior in the future.

To be effective, intervention must be swift—occurring at the moment of misbehavior—and it must be sure—suited to the misbehavior. The term "swift" doesn't imply "impulsive." We need to be prepared to act quickly but with reasoned effort, maintaining a noncombative attitude while moving to immediately end the misbehavior. A "sure" intervention is one that's appropriate to the goal of the misbehavior. For example, a time-out technique would be suitable to use with students seeking power, but for students trying to avoid failure, time-out would provide just what they want—a release from a situation they don't want to be in anyway.

"Consistent" is another watchword that applies to interventions. We're being consistent when we intervene every time the student misbehaves; however, the intervention need not be the same one time after time. Many intervention techniques are suggested as part of the *Cooperative Discipline* process. Having a variety of techniques to choose from gives you lots of options, flexibility, and confidence. Some of the ideas may be new to you; others may be familiar. No technique presented is inherently better than any other; each can be useful in the right circumstance.

Choose first the techniques that make the most sense to you, that seem to fit your teaching style and personality, that are relatively easy to apply, and that are particularly appropriate to your students. Then try other techniques as needed. Most of the suggested techniques are adaptable for use with students of any age, from kindergarten through high school. A few of the techniques are useful with only one age group, and these are specified as such.

Intervention techniques tailored to each of the four goals of misbehavior are described in Chapters 6, 9, 10, 11, and 13.

Step 4: Select Encouragement Techniques to Build Self-Esteem

If we were to conclude a School Action Plan at Step 3, we could anticipate that the student would misbehave again—today, tomorrow, or the next day. Intervention is only a stopgap measure that ends misbehavior in progress but doesn't prevent future misbehavior. It must be accompanied by encouragement techniques that build self-esteem, which strengthens the motivation to cooperate and learn. The building blocks of self-esteem are the same three Cs that help students feel they belong (Concept 2 of Chapter 2). When students believe they are *capable* and know they can *connect* and *contribute* successfully, they no longer need to misbehave in a mistaken attempt to fulfill their need to belong.

At Step 4, then, we plot encouragement techniques—ways in which we can assure the student that he or she is capable, can connect, and can contribute. No crystal ball is necessary to help us predict what techniques we'll be able to use and when. By thinking about past experiences with the student, we can usually recall some positive behaviors, and these can head our list of behaviors to be reinforced with encouragement statements. As we observe other positive behaviors, we can add them and their matching encouragements to the list.

Encouragement techniques are neither time-consuming nor difficult to learn. We simply need to become aware of them and make a commitment to using them daily. The more they're used, the more naturally they'll occur in our interactions with the student. Such reinforcing behavior on our part can transform our relationship with the student. We'll probably find ourselves acting more positively toward the student because we're starting to expect good things from him or her. In turn, the student's perception of how to achieve belonging will change course as his or her self-esteem is boosted.

Chapters 14 through 16 describe specific techniques for encouraging students to connect, to contribute, and to feel capable.

Step 5: Involve Parents as Partners

Last, but not least in importance, the redirection of the student's behavior becomes a joint effort of both teacher and parents—a partnership that educators have long claimed is vital to the discipline process. Under Step 5, we can list the ways we'll ask parents to cooperate with us in working with their daughter or son. These are some of the options that invite parent participation:

- Notify parents that a School Action Plan has been developed, and ask for their comments. We've probably involved the parents already by means of conferences, phone calls, and notes to communicate our concerns about their child's behavior. Presenting a plan to parents is concrete evidence of our concern and our willingness to work with them and their child.

- Invite parents to join us in the process of developing a School Action Plan, since they can offer helpful insights into what works with their child.

- Help parents develop a Home Action Plan similar to the School Action Plan. This plan provides parents with a variety of strategies they could use at home to mirror and reinforce those being used at school.

- Invite parents to participate in a parent education program that the school may sponsor.

- Invite parents to make use of any parent education resources that the school may provide.

Further information about each of these options is given in Chapter 17 of this handbook.

Cooperation: The Password to Designing a School Action Plan

A School Action Plan enables the idea of cooperation to become an actuality. In designing a plan, we confirm our willingness to try to cooperate with the student to effect change. We are recognizing that the student needs help in choosing positive behavior, and we are committing ourselves to giving that help in specific ways.

Cooperation also becomes an actuality when we invite other teachers who deal with the student to join us in the process of creating a School Action Plan. This cooperative brainstorming can provide new insight into teacher-student interactions, especially if the student exhibits Jekyll-and-Hyde behavior, behaving appropriately in one teacher's classroom and misbehaving in another's. Why does Mr. García describe Jesse as "well-adjusted and studious" while Ms. Herrold describes Jesse as "disruptive and lazy"? A plan for Jesse would be incomplete without the input of *both* Mr. García and Ms. Herrold.

Counselors, psychologists, social workers, and administrators are others who can be asked to help develop a School Action Plan. Since they are not directly involved in any of the classroom interactions that are causing problems, they can provide neutral advice concerning intervention and encouragement techniques. Moreover, these specialists can assist in efforts to involve parents as partners in the discipline process. Suggestions for enlisting the help of these specialists are given in Chapter 17.

Some students present more challenges than others.

The invitation to cooperate in designing a School Action Plan can also be extended to a student at any level—from kindergarten on up. Of course, the younger the student, the smaller the role. When dealing with power and revenge behaviors, young students can be given the choice of two or three consequences selected ahead of time by the teacher. High school students can have a greater say in negotiating solutions and choosing consequences. The more voice and choice students have, the more cooperative and responsible they'll act and feel.

By requesting a student's insight, we're not only signaling that we care but also boosting the student's self-esteem; we're transmitting the belief that the student is capable of making a valuable contribution. Moreover, by inviting student participation, we're putting some of the responsibility for solving behavior problems where it belongs—on the student. Of course, when we ask the student to help design the plan, we're also telling the student that we're prepared to help shoulder the responsibility. We're committing ourselves to interacting positively with the student, as opposed to reacting negatively to the student's misbehavior.

Some young people are real pros at playing home against school. Teacher gets one story; parents get another. We can end this game when we invite both student and parents to develop a School Action Plan with us. Once students understand that both parents and teacher are determined to end the misbehavior in a systematic way, they realize that it's time to make a change. All too often, young people think that a teacher's purpose for calling a conference is to get them into trouble with their parents. When students realize that the real purpose is to solve a problem in a firm but friendly way, the door swings open for creating a positive teacher-student relationship. Guidelines for involving parents and students in conferences are given in Chapter 17.

The School Action Plan as a Monitor of Progress

A School Action Plan should be a living document subject to change. We can review it once or twice a week, noting how the selected interventions and encouragement techniques affect our interactions with the student. Unsuccessful techniques can be deleted and new ones added. Comments and suggestions from others involved as partners in the plan can be incorporated. Although the plan is structured in steps as an aid to focusing effort, it also invites the flexibility necessary to determine unique solutions to specific behavior problems.

The Process Starts—Step by Step

Writing a sample School Action Plan as you're introduced to the *Cooperative Discipline* process through the chapters in this handbook is a helpful learning experience. As you design a plan, you'll be able to see firsthand how the process translates into practical action.

As the subject of the plan, select a student whose behavior has been disturbing you recently, but don't choose the student who is giving you the hardest time in class. After all, if you were taking a course in woodworking, your first project would be a simple shelf, not a dining room hutch! Give yourself an easy start as you begin to learn the process, thereby assuring yourself of a successful first model for change. Once you've taken the steps for someone who is third or fourth on your list of misbehaving students, you'll have the confidence you need to begin tackling the tough ones!

Taking Objective Action

Step 1: Pinpoint and Describe the Student's Behavior

Writing descriptions of a student's problem behavior is our first step in designing a *Cooperative Discipline* School Action Plan. The plan's success hinges on the accuracy of our descriptions. If we observe and record the student's behavior objectively, we'll be able to determine the goal of the misbehavior (Step 2) and choose relevant intervention and encouragement techniques (Steps 3 and 4). Moreover, we'll be able to communicate effectively with the student's parents (Step 5). This chapter presents guidelines on how to achieve the objectivity that is crucial not only to Step 1 of the School Action Plan but also to the entire plan.

The Key to Accuracy: Gather and State Facts

Just as newspaper reporters need to gather facts before they can write an accurate story, so we need to gather facts before we can describe a student's behavior objectively. A comprehensive description includes exactly *what* the student does to misbehave, *when* the student usually does it, and approximately *how often* the student does it.

Avoid Subjective Terms

The *what* of misbehavior needs to be a straightforward statement with no subjective garnishes. Our natural tendency is to view misbehavior in terms of how it affects us or in relation to our expectations of how a student should behave. To achieve the desired objectivity, we need to train ourselves to become impartial observers. Otherwise, we run the risk of biasing not only our own relationship with the student but also that of others who deal with the student. For example, consider the inherent bias that marks each of these statements:

- Jim is totally impossible. I don't know what to do with him.
- Jane is so scattered. Pray you don't get her next year!
- Jason is so immature.
- Julian is one of the most uncooperative kids I've ever had.
- Jolinda is so disruptive. She drives me crazy!

Expectations and past experiences can sometimes cloud our perceptions.

The descriptors used—*impossible, scattered, immature, uncooperative, disruptive*—affect teachers almost as negatively as the behaviors themselves. While the words allow the speakers to let off steam, they also relate personal opinions that the students' behaviors are beyond redemption. For example, by calling Jolinda disruptive, her teacher is not only personally interpreting Jolinda's behavior but also expressing a hopeless attitude about figuring out how to help Jolinda change her behavior. "Disruptive" is a general, negative label that expresses a value judgment instead of focusing on what Jolinda does to misbehave. Moreover, if Jolinda tunes in to her teacher's attitude, the label "disruptive" could become a self-fulfilling prophecy. When we perceive students as disruptive, we may treat them as if we always expect them to act disruptively, and they may act accordingly.

Labels used to describe students' behavior can also transmit negative expectations to other teachers. When Jane walks into Mr. Fox's homeroom next fall, he may anticipate the worst because she's been portrayed as "scattered." Similarly, the use of subjective, evaluative terms can jeopardize the help requested when students with behavior problems are referred to other school personnel. If the school counselor receives an evaluation stating that "Jason is so immature," the counselor won't be able to help either Jason or his teacher change the situation. The counselor needs to know exactly what Jason is doing to give his teacher the impression of immaturity. Only with that information can a specific plan be designed to encourage Jason to eliminate the behavior.

Subjective statements and labels also tend to obscure the fact that a student may behave differently for different teachers. Two teachers may describe Jim's behavior as "impossible"; four others may view Jim as "well-adjusted, inquisitive, and studious." Moreover, what one teacher perceives as "inquisitive" behavior may be described by another as "impossible" behavior. For example, the social studies teacher might regard Jim as inquisitive because he asks a lot of questions and constantly suggests alternative interpretations. Jim's English teacher might describe the same behavior as impossible.

When describing behavior, we can avoid making subjective statements and assigning labels, by using emotionally neutral, objective terms. Consider these restatements of the previous subjective descriptions:

- Jim sticks his foot in the aisle and trips other second graders about five times each day.
- Jane fails to hand in English assignments at least three days each week.
- Jason rocks back and forth in his chair during science and taps his pencil on his desk during quizzes and tests.
- When asked to complete his worksheets, Julian makes comments such as "You can't make me do this" and "I'm going to do something else instead."
- Jolinda talks to other students about seven times during history lectures. When asked to stop, she mutters a response under her breath.

These statements portray behaviors in impersonal, unemotional terms. Instead of interpreting the behaviors, they focus on what actually happens and when it happens.

Record Frequency of Behavior

Besides describing behaviors objectively, the previous statements also include information about *how often* a behavior occurs. When we're having difficulty with a student, we tend to think that a behavior occurs more frequently than it actually does. For example, we may be convinced that Eva taps her pencil "continuously." If we were to document the frequency of the behavior over several days, we might be surprised to discover that Eva taps her pencil an average of only four times, and only during social studies.

Another problem with using terms such as *seldom, usually, often, occasionally, frequently,* and *once in a while* is that they mean different things to different people. For example, the statement "Ethan is constantly out of his seat" can be interpreted in various ways. It may mean that Ethan does not sit down from 9:00 A.M. to 3:00 P.M., that he pops up and walks around the room ten times every hour, or that he goes to the drinking fountain five or six times a day.

Only when we view troubling behavior in terms of *what, when,* and *how often* are we able to describe it objectively. Such an impartial viewpoint enables us to recognize that changing our interactions with a student is possible, that we can help a student choose more appropriate behavior. No interventions or encouragement techniques can alleviate "impossible behavior"; however, there are interventions and encouragement techniques that can help convince Vana to get to class on time and Vince to quit bullying younger children on the playground.

Double-Check Objectivity

Here's an easy way to determine if we're describing behavior objectively: If our words say no more and no less than could be recorded by a video camera or a tape recorder, our description is probably accurate. Since electronic equipment can't document such subjective evaluations as "disrespectful" or "uncooperative," our descriptions should be free of such terms.

Suppose Claudia stares out the window during math class. A video camera could capture her face turned toward the window and her eyes gazing outside, but it couldn't capture her thoughts. If we were to judge that she is "daydreaming," we might be right or we might be wrong. Claudia might be dreaming of a romantic

Sometimes a coworker can help us regain objectivity.

encounter with the cute fellow in the second row, or she might be thinking about a math problem. We simply don't know what's going on inside of Claudia's head. Therefore, an objective description of her behavior would be "She stares out the window."

Clinton may disrupt his neighbors, but exactly how? A video camera could record him passing notes, tapping another student's shoulder, and throwing paper airplanes. These behaviors as well as when and how often he does them would comprise objective descriptions.

Take Step 1: Pinpoint and Describe the Student's Behavior

Keeping in mind the guidelines given in the previous sections, observe the student you've selected as the subject of your sample School Action Plan for several days. Under Step 1 of the plan, record the behaviors that disturb you the most as well as when and how often they occur. For example, you might note on Monday that "Celia takes about twenty minutes to write her name on a reading worksheet and to start work." This statement could then be checkmarked each time Celia repeats the behavior during the next few days. Your descriptions of behaviors may also include quotes from the student, such as this statement: "Cedric replied 'Make me' when asked to participate in a history discussion."

Because you're specifically tracking the behavior of a Celia or a Cedric, you'll probably have a fairly complete set of descriptions by the end of the observation period. "Fairly complete" is satisfactory because that's all that's achievable. Unfortunately, you can't hit a pause button to freeze class activity so that you can immediately record each incident of inappropriate behavior. You'll usually have to postpone writing descriptions until the end of class or even the end of the teaching day, and you may forget a few. Reliance on memory may be unscientific, but it's the best you can do since you're probably dealing with twenty or more other students besides Celia or Cedric!

2

SECTION TWO

Taking Corrective Action: Attention-Seeking Behavior

Attention-seeking students are like stage performers; they require an audience. In the lower grades, the attention seekers usually gear their performance to the teacher. As these students move into the upper grades, especially high school, they prefer a wider audience. They usually perform as much for their classmates as for their teachers. Some ambitiously covet the rewards of the virtuoso attention-getting performance, gaining the notice of guidance counselors, administrators, and perhaps the entire school community.

CHAPTER 5
Characteristics of Attention-Seeking Behavior

Many misbehaving students are seeking extra attention. Note the term *extra*. We all need a certain amount of attention to feel that we belong, to know that we're an important part of our social group. (Recall Concept 2 in Chapter 2.) In contrast, students who misbehave for attention are never satisfied with a normal amount. They want more and more, as if they carry around with them a bucket labeled "attention" that they expect the teacher to fill. There's a hole in the bucket, however, so that no matter how much attention is put in, it seeps out. Since their bucket is never full, these students continue to misbehave.

Attention-seeking students are like stage performers; they require an audience. In the lower grades, the attention seekers usually gear their performance to the teacher. As these students move into the upper grades, especially high school, they prefer a wider audience. They usually perform as much for their classmates as for their teachers. Some ambitiously covet the rewards of the virtuoso attention-getting performance, gaining the notice of guidance counselors, administrators, and perhaps the entire school community.

Active Attention-Seeking Behavior

Attention-seeking students are equipped with tricks I call "attention-getting mechanisms" (AGMs). For instance, second-grader Jeremiah Jensen has 101 AGMs. He taps his pencil on his desk, talks out of turn, trips classmates on the way to the washroom, wiggles his left ear while sticking out his tongue, uses four-letter words that his teacher didn't learn until college, and constantly pleads for help while his classmates quietly finish assignments. Jeremiah's sister Jenny, a sophomore in high school, also has many AGMs. She regularly saunters into class ten minutes late, combs her hair in class, passes notes to friends across the room, and asks irrelevant questions during lectures.

Active AGMs are unmistakable. These misbehaviors disrupt the class and prevent us from teaching. If we don't take immediate corrective action, we risk losing control of the classroom.

Although an infinite variety of AGMs exist, each type doesn't require a different response. Once Jeremiah's and Jenny's teachers learn to deal effectively with attention-seeking behavior, the number and value of the two students' AGMs will gradually decrease.

Some bids for attention are less than subtle.

Passive Attention-Seeking Behavior

Passive attention-seeking students also employ AGMs. Unlike the active variety, however, passive AGMs rarely disrupt the entire class. We may falsely think, "Thank heavens no one is misbehaving right now. I can proceed with today's lesson." We fail to see, or perhaps we ignore, the passive attention seeker until the misbehavior gets under our skin or until we realize that the student's ability to learn has diminished or until we're able to find a moment to try to do something.

I like to describe passive AGMs as "one-pea-at-a-time" behavior. Did you ever watch a parent feeding a reluctant toddler? "Here, Penelope, eat one pea for Aunt Patti. Now take another for Uncle Pete. How about one for Polly?" Three hours later, parent and child are still at the table, with seven more peas to go.

We see this one-pea-at-a-time behavior in students whose reaction time works only on slow, slower, and slowest speeds. These students are the dawdlers, the ones who haven't opened their math books while the rest of the class has already finished the third problem. We feel like shaking some life into them, although we know from observing them outside of class that they really can move and react normally.

Redirecting passive AGMs is generally more difficult than redirecting active ones. Passive students often respond to attempts to get them moving by saying, "How come you're scolding me? I'm not doing anything wrong or bothering anybody." In contrast, the misbehavior of children who actively seek attention is so obvious that they can't deny their actions so easily.

Teacher and Student Response Clues

Teacher Response to Behavior

We have a built-in mechanism that spontaneously identifies misbehavior—our emotional gauge. At the moment of misbehavior, two readings of our emotional gauge can serve as clues to identifying the goal of the misbehavior: first, determine our feelings about the misbehavior, and then consider our initial action impulse, or how we would stop the misbehavior if we didn't think before acting.

Attention-seeking behavior usually sparks feelings of irritation or annoyance. The emotional response is fairly mild since this is not the worst kind of misbehavior, and students typically respond fairly quickly to corrective methods. An initial action impulse tends to be verbal, using words to coax the student to end the misbehavior, to reprimand the student, or to lecture the student.

Student Response to Intervention

Student response to our attempts to stop the misbehavior can provide clues for identifying the goal of the misbehavior. Attention-seeking students usually act compliantly when we intervene. This makes sense because the purpose of their misbehavior is to get our attention. Once they receive their payoff, their need to continue misbehaving is gone—at least for the moment. The students therefore stop misbehaving temporarily.

Origins of Attention-Seeking Behavior

Parents and Teachers Reward Misbehavior with Attention

How do children learn they can get more attention from adults by misbehaving than by behaving? My hunch is that the lesson begins in infancy. Babies cry, and moms and dads come running. Babies amuse themselves happily, and parents tend to stay away, enjoying a rare moment of peace. As babies become toddlers, they learn that if they touch the crystal bowl on the coffee table, they receive immediate attention. If they play contentedly with their blocks, however, they're usually ignored for a time. Childhood experiences like these reinforce the conclusion that "all I need to do to keep Mom and Dad busy with me is to do something they've told me not to do." The attention gained is negative attention, but negative attention is far better than no attention at all.

The desire for negative attention can also be fostered unwittingly by teachers in everyday classroom situations. Jonathan is sitting quietly in the back row, completing the practice geometry problems. Meanwhile, Jill is talking loudly to a girl across the aisle, disrupting at least a dozen classmates. Who does Mrs. Muñoz speak to? Jill, of course!

Children Don't Know How to Ask for Attention Appropriately

Another circumstance that fosters attention-seeking behavior is the gap found in almost all children's education: No one teaches children how to ask for attention in an appropriate manner when they believe they need it.

Attention is a basic psychological need, just as food is a basic physical need. Children are taught to recognize when they are physically hungry and to ask for food instead of simply wailing. Why not also teach them to recognize when they're psychologically hungry and to ask for attention? If this were taught, the need to misbehave for attention would diminish greatly. Students might come into the classroom with requests such as these: "Mr. Burlingham, I'm feeling low and need a little extra attention today" or "Could the class please give me one minute of undivided attention right now? I really need a boost today."

Additional Causes

Most educators would agree that the number of students who misbehave for attention appears to be increasing. Is this because children receive less personal attention at home these days? Has the demise of the extended family deprived children of so much interpersonal contact outside school that they substitute attention from counselors and teachers for the attention they used to receive from grandparents, aunts, uncles, and cousins? Perhaps too many hours spent in front of the TV contribute to the problem. As schools have grown larger and class sizes have increased, maybe the only way students can get a reasonable amount of attention from school personnel is by misbehaving.

Attention-Seeking Behavior's Silver Lining

Attention-seeking behavior does have a silver lining. Students who seek a teacher's attention are at least showing they want a relationship with the teacher; they just don't know how to connect in a positive way. Most teachers would rather deal with a student demanding attention than with a zombie who doesn't care about anything or anyone.

If we recall this silver lining every time a student misbehaves for attention, our annoyance and irritation probably will diminish. By understanding the basic need to belong and recognizing that a child associates misbehavior with getting attention, we'll be able to take effective action.

Principles of Prevention

Two general principles can guide our efforts to prevent attention-seeking behavior in our classroom. The first is to give lots of attention for appropriate behavior—two, three, even ten times more attention for positive behavior than for misbehavior. The second is to teach students to ask directly for extra attention when they think they need it. Chapter 15 discusses how to apply both of these principles.

Take Step 2: Identify the Goal of the Misbehavior

The goal of the student's misbehavior is entered under Step 2 of the School Action Plan. To determine whether the student employs attention-seeking behavior, use the Chapter 5 Chart as a guide to evaluating the behavior descriptions that you've listed under Step 1 of the plan. This chart summarizes the key information about attention-seeking behavior that's presented in this chapter.

The teacher and student response clues are most helpful in deciding whether attention is the goal of misbehavior. Take note of your feelings and your initial action impulse when the student misbehaves, and also how the student responds when you intervene to stop the behavior. The teacher and student response clues to each of the four goals of misbehavior are summarized in Appendix B, Teacher and Student Response Clues to Identifying the Goal of Misbehavior, a handy reference for double-checking identification of a particular goal.

Active Attention-Seeking Behavior	*Active AGMs:* Student does all kinds of behaviors that distract teacher and classmates.
Passive Attention-Seeking Behavior	*Passive AGMs:* Student exhibits one-pea-at-a-time behavior, operates on slow, slower, slowest speeds.
Teacher Response to Behavior	*Feelings:* Irritation, annoyance.
	Action impulse: Verbal.
Student Response to Intervention	*Response style:* Compliant.
	Response action: Stops misbehavior temporarily.
Origins of Behavior	Parents and teachers tend to pay more attention to misbehavior than to appropriate behavior.
	Children aren't taught how to ask for attention appropriately.
	Children may be deprived of sufficient personal attention.
Silver Lining	Student wants a relationship with the teacher (and classmates).
Principles of Prevention	Give lots of attention for appropriate behavior.
	Teach student to ask directly for extra attention when needed.

Investigating Attention-Seeking Behavior

1 Give some examples of active and passive attention-seeking behaviors that you've observed in your classroom.

_____

_____

_____

_____

2 Do you agree with the suggested origins of attention-seeking behavior? Why or why not?

_____

_____

_____

3 The silver lining in attention-seeking behavior is that students show they want a relationship with the teacher. Do you agree with this statement? Why or why not?

_____

_____

_____

4 Complete this sentence: When I was a child, one way I got extra attention at home or

school was _____

_____

_____

_____

When the Goal Is Attention: Interventions

Six Intervention Strategies

In this chapter, we'll explore many intervention techniques useful with students who choose to misbehave for attention. The techniques are grouped under six general strategies.

Strategy 1: Minimize the Attention

We walk a fine line when students misbehave for attention. Giving them too much attention reinforces their mistaken notion that they can experience belonging only when they receive extra notice. On the other hand, we have to discourage such behavior when it disturbs our teaching and distracts other students from learning. Under this general strategy of minimizing attention are a variety of techniques that can help us convince students to stop attention-seeking behavior without our reinforcing it.

Ignore the behavior. Often, the best way to minimize attention-seeking behavior is to refuse to react to it. Our nonresponse wipes away the payoff that students expect—extra attention.

When students misbehave for attention, we can ask ourselves this question: What would happen if I ignored the behavior instead of interfering? If the answer is that only the attention seeker would be inconvenienced and no one else would be affected, ignoring the misbehavior is likely to be an effective technique. When students don't receive the anticipated attention, they'll usually abandon their efforts after a few tries.

Give "The Eye." "Stare them down," recommends a savvy seventh-grade teacher. "They know what they're doing, they know you know what they're doing, and they know that 'The Eye' means 'stop.'" Eye contact is the only attention that students receive with this technique. No words—just looks.

Stand close by. Physical proximity is another tool that helps minimize attention-seeking behavior. While continuing with the lesson at hand, the teacher

Eye contact can do a lot to discourage irritating behavior.

simply moves to stand next to the misbehaving student. No eye contact is made, and nothing is said. The student's efforts are usually discouraged when the teacher's presence is so immediate.

Mention the student's name while teaching. This technique gives minimum recognition to the misbehavior while communicating that the student should stop the behavior and attend to what's being taught. The teacher does this by periodically inserting the student's name into the context of the lesson. Here's what this might sound like: "Now during this period—Melissa—in American history, the settlers . . ." This technique also can be used in conjunction with The Eye or with standing next to the student.

Send a secret signal. Teachers have been using signals for years. For example, most students know that a teacher's upheld hand with two fingers raised or crossed means "quiet down." We can easily establish other similar signals to give to young children who misbehave frequently.

Consider my experience with Barry, a second grader who interrupted me during lessons. One day, in desperation, I asked Barry, "What do I have to do to keep you quiet while I'm busy with other children?" Barry responded by making a motion with his hands as though he were squeezing an imaginary basketball. "What does that mean?" I asked him. "It means 'get it together,'" Barry replied.

Then and there, Barry and I made an agreement that whenever I gave him that squeeze signal, he would stop whatever he was doing and get back to work. Believe it or not, the strange signal worked! I'd often add a wink when making the sign. Barry would smile and settle down, satisfied that he'd had two seconds of my time just for him. For years afterward, whenever he'd pass me in the hall or on the playground, Barry would make our secret signal. That I'd cared enough to share the signal with him continued to make our relationship special.

Give written notice. Since we know that tomorrow we'll be faced with students misbehaving for attention, we can prepare today by duplicating a stack of notes that give this message: Please stop what you are doing right now. When students interrupt for attention, we can just drop one of these notes on their desk. We don't need to utter a word since the note says it all. This technique works particularly well with older children.

Give an I-message. There are times when we just want to say "Stop!" to a student who is disrupting the classroom. Psychologists tell us that the most effective way to do this is to deliver an "I-message" to the student. This verbal statement gives specific information about the misbehavior and its effect on others. Here's an example of an I-message: "Cornelia, when you talk to your neighbor during class discussions, I get annoyed because I lose my train of thought. Please stop."

Notice there are four parts to the preceding I-message. First, it contains an objective description of the disruptive behavior: "When you talk to your neighbor . . ." Second, it relates the teacher's feeling: "I get annoyed . . ." The third part tells the effect of the misbehavior on the teacher or on the class: ". . . because I lose my train of thought." The final part is a request: "Please stop."

I-messages tell students exactly how we feel. With attention-seeking behaviors, talking about our feelings in this brief way doesn't become a payoff for misbehavior. As long as we don't add body language to our words, we'll find that such statements can influence many students to stop what they're doing.

Strategy 2: Legitimize the Behavior

A fascination with forbidden fruit seems to be intrinsic to human nature. Just as Adam and Eve couldn't resist doing what they were told not to do, many students succumb to temptation. We can't stop them from biting the apple, but we can take away all the fun by using several clever techniques that legitimize the behavior.

Make a lesson out of the behavior. Here's an example that a junior high teacher shared with me:

> *The students in Mr. Hardy's science class seemed to be obsessed with spitballs. None of the usual methods for banishing spitballs worked, so Mr. Hardy decided to legitimize the behavior. He told the class that since they loved spitballs so much, he was going to teach an entire unit on spitballs. He had the class plot trajectories, do time and distance studies, and keep copious notes on their experiments. By the time the three-week unit was finished, the students wanted nothing more to do with spitballs!*

This technique can be adapted to many situations. For example, the use of inappropriate language might be discouraged by assigning etymology reports.

Extend the behavior to its most extreme form. Another alternative that Mr. Hardy might have used to cleanse his class of spitballs is this:

The offenders could be assigned the task of making 500 spitballs. Before they've made the first 100, they'll wish they'd never seen a spitball. The boredom of the task, coupled with an increasingly parched throat, will convince the students that making spitballs is not all it's cracked up to be.

This technique is effective with many harmless yet annoying behaviors. For instance, students who don't stay in their seats can be requested to stand for the entire period, and students who talk constantly can be required to fill an hour-long audiocassette with their words.

Have the whole class join in the behavior. Simon is tapping his pencil on his desk—again. "Okay, class, pick up your pencils and tap them for the next three minutes." With everyone participating in the misbehavior, Simon loses his payoff: he's not getting any special attention from anyone. Since pencil tapping has become legitimate, the fun has vanished.

Using this technique may cost us several minutes of teaching time, but remember that whenever we're interrupted by an annoying behavior, we also lose teaching time. Isn't it better to do something that's likely to end a misbehavior than to spend a minute or two daily trying to correct it?

Use a diminishing quota. This technique is recommended by Dr. Rudolf Dreikurs in *Psychology in the Classroom*.[1] It involves allowing incidents of particular misbehaviors to occur, but only in the number agreed on beforehand and with the stipulation that the number will decrease daily.

For an example of how this technique works, consider how it might be applied to convince Johnny to choose different behavior. Johnny burps loudly at least a dozen times during each civics class. One morning, in a private conversation with Johnny, his teacher negotiates how many burps will be allowed in class that day. If the mutually selected number is fewer than Johnny's usual number of burps, the situation already will have improved slightly. Each time Johnny burps, his teacher just smiles at him and makes a slash mark in the corner of the chalkboard. When Johnny reaches his quota for the day, the teacher shrugs and gestures "That's it" to him. The teacher and Johnny continue negotiating a lower number each day until the behavior disappears.

Physical proximity is another tool that helps minimize
attention-seeking behavior.

The skeptics are probably saying, "Wait a minute. What if a student goes over the quota?" If that happens, abandon this technique and substitute another suggested in this section, or analyze the misbehavior again to see if its goal might be power instead of attention. The technique of using a diminishing quota works only with attention-seeking behaviors.

Teachers who've used this technique report that most students adhere to the quota. Why? Because the private conversation, the smiles, and the slash marks provide all the needed attention. The students are not in a power struggle with us, so they don't really need or want to challenge our authority. They just want that bit of attention that makes them feel they belong.

Strategy 3: Do the Unexpected

Frequently, we can end attention-seeking behavior by doing the unexpected. When we do the unexpected, we're giving this message: "I see you and know what you are doing, but I'm not going to play your game." Since the game of misbehavior requires at least two players, it's just about over when the teacher withdraws.

The more humor we can use when doing the unexpected, the better. A quick laugh relieves tension and refreshes the atmosphere, making it easy for learning to resume. Garrison Keillor says, "Humor is a presence in the world—like grace—and shines on everybody." The more humor shines in our classroom at the moment of misbehavior, the more quickly and easily the moment will pass.

Turn out the lights. This is an old standby that teachers have used for years. When a student or an entire class gets out of hand, simply flick off the wall switch and wait silently for a few moments. No need to give Lecture 385 on what the students are doing wrong; they know when they're misbehaving. In this situation, silence speaks louder than words.

Play a musical sound. Music teachers and primary teachers often play a chord or a progression of chords on the piano at the moment of misbehavior. If there's no piano handy, we can use any kind of instrument that appeals to us—a bell, cymbals, a tambourine.

Lower your voice. Several years ago, I made an informal survey in which I asked students this question: "What do you dislike most about school?" The most frequent response—teachers who yell.

Yelling when students misbehave not only adds another dimension to the confusion already in the classroom but also reduces the students' sense of belonging and their self-esteem. When we lower our voice, however, students have to pay attention and strain to hear us, which distracts them from misbehaving. When we talk quietly, they talk quietly, creating a productive classroom atmosphere for all.

Change your voice. Use unusual speech patterns, sounds, accents, or languages—even gibberish. Chant or sing words, talk in a monotone, speak in a high pitch or a low pitch, or mix the two. Any of these vocal changes will distract students misbehaving for attention.

Some teachers find a secret signal to be effective.

Talk to the wall. This technique was reported to me by a middle school teacher. When one or more of her students are misbehaving for attention, she walks over to a wall and begins a monologue: "Oh, Wall, you wouldn't believe what is happening in my room just now. Someone is calling out without raising her hand. Someone else is tipping back on his chair. Will you just look at the student who is throwing paper airplanes in the back of the room? Please, Wall, don't just stand there. Help me with this bunch of kids."

If you decide to try this technique, you might want to warn your principal in advance that you talk to walls. Otherwise, the principal may decide you're a candidate for a psychological leave!

Use one-liners. Any quick quip will distract the misbehaving student, as long as it's uttered in fun, without a hint of sarcasm. One fourth-grade teacher has a magic vacuum cleaner. As an immediate response to a misbehavior, he often says, "Wait a minute. Here comes my magic vacuum cleaner to suck you up." Another teacher says, "Watch out! Here come twenty lashes with a wet noodle!"

Cease teaching temporarily. Students know we're in school to teach. When we interrupt a lesson to "do nothing" for a few minutes, we send students a powerful message to change their behavior. We can do nothing by standing silently near the chalkboard or by sitting down at our desk to read. "Let me know when you're ready to resume the lesson" is all we have to say. Peer pressure will soon go to work, and, before long, peace and quiet will prevail.

Strategy 4: Distract the Student

No one can do two things at once for very long. Therefore, we can distract students from continuing inappropriate behavior by focusing their attention elsewhere.

Ask a direct question. The moment of misbehavior is a fine time to ask the student a direct question such as "Raymond, what are the instructions I just gave?" or "Rhonda, how would you tackle this physics problem?" Questions like these not only distract students from their misbehavior but also focus their attention on the lesson at hand. For extra emphasis, combine this technique with one of those suggested under the heading "Strategy 1: Minimize the Attention," earlier in this chapter.

Ask a favor. "Garfield, please collect everyone's essay." "Gertrude, would you mind taking the attendance sheet to the office right now?" "Garry, go to Ms. Gargin's room and ask if she could spare a couple of pieces of chalk for us." Smart students might begin viewing the request of a favor as their reward for misbehaving, if this technique is used too often. As an occasional technique, however, it works just fine.

Change the activity. If many students are misbehaving simultaneously in a bid for attention, a change of activity usually distracts them from their misbehavior. Ask them to clear their desks, to listen to new instructions, or to take out different books.

Strategy 5: Notice Appropriate Behavior

Rather than speak directly to a student who is misbehaving and thereby reinforce the behavior with our attention, we can say something positive to a classmate who is sitting near the student and behaving appropriately. In this way, we convey the message that good behavior, not misbehavior, receives a payoff.

Thank students. We can thank a student who is doing just what we want the misbehaving student to be doing: "Thank you, Juanita, for having your math book open to the correct page and your eyes focused on the board." "Thanks, June, for keeping your hands to yourself and your feet under your chair." Such statements relay exactly what behavior is expected of the misbehaving student.

This technique works only if we describe the desired behavior in objective terms. General statements such as "Thanks, Juanita, for being so good" or "Thanks, June, for doing what you're supposed to do" are ineffective because they don't clearly communicate our expectations. Be careful to avoid thanking the same students too often, or they'll be set up as teacher's pets and resented by their classmates.

Write well-behaved students' names on the chalkboard. We can write the names of those students who are behaving appropriately on the chalkboard. By doing this, we're not only reinforcing good behavior but also sending a subtle message to misbehaving students to stop.

Strategy 6: Move the Student

Most attention seekers like to have an audience. When we remove such students from their audience, we're taking away some of their reward, which inclines them to end the misbehavior. Two techniques are effective for accomplishing this.

Legitimizing misbehavior puts teachers at a distinct advantage.

Change the student's seat. Sometimes a change of seat is all that's needed: "Earl, please move to the empty seat in the third row." Continue the lesson while Earl moves, so he doesn't receive any undue class attention. Even though such attention would be embarrassing, Earl still might consider it a reward for his misbehavior.

Send the student to the thinking chair. Some teachers place a "thinking chair" in a quiet area of the room, out of the direct line of vision between the teacher and the rest of the class. The thinking chair in my classroom was an old wicker chair that I'd picked up at a flea market and painted purple. Any chair that's handy will do, as long as it doesn't resemble the other chairs in the classroom.

The purpose of this chair is to provide a spot where misbehaving students can think about how they will act differently when they return to their seats. Five minutes in the chair is generally enough time. The rest of the class should understand that someone in the thinking chair is never to be disturbed.

All we need say to a misbehaving student is, "Evangeline, please go sit in the thinking chair." If Evangeline doesn't move quietly to the chair, she may be seeking power rather than attention. Likewise, if Evangeline misbehaves again when her time in the chair is up, her goal is probably power. A different technique is then necessary.

Take Step 3: Choose Intervention Techniques

If you've determined that the student who's the subject of your School Action Plan has attention as his or her goal, select several of the intervention techniques described in this chapter and listed in the Chapter 6 Chart. Make your choices on the basis of these factors:

- the student's age
- what makes the most sense to you
- what fits your teaching style and personality

Record the selected techniques under Step 3 of the plan.

As you complete this step, keep in mind that intervention does not mean punishment. Instead, think of intervention as guidance with a double purpose: to stop the behavior occurring at the moment and to influence the student to choose more appropriate behavior in the future.

A summary chart that includes interventions recommended for each of the four goals of misbehavior is presented in Appendix C, Summary Chart of Interventions.

Note

1. Rudolf Dreikurs, *Psychology in the Classroom* (New York: Harper & Row, 1957, 1968), 141-142.

Interventions for Attention-Seeking Behavior

General Strategy	Techniques
Minimize the attention.	Ignore the behavior. Give "The Eye." Stand close by. Mention the student's name while teaching. Send a secret signal. Give written notice. Give an I-message.
Legitimize the behavior.	Make a lesson out of the behavior. Extend the behavior to its most extreme form. Have the whole class join in the behavior. Use a diminishing quota.
Do the unexpected.	Turn out the lights. Play a musical sound. Lower your voice. Change your voice. Talk to the wall. Use one-liners. Cease teaching temporarily.
Distract the student.	Ask a direct question. Ask a favor. Change the activity.
Notice appropriate behavior.	Thank students. Write well-behaved students' names on the chalkboard.
Move the student.	Change the student's seat. Send the student to the thinking chair.

Interventions for Attention-Seeking Behavior

Below are the interventions suggested for attention-seeking behavior. Next to each, write the symbols that are correct for you:

    * Indicates interventions you are currently using
    A Indicates interventions that are appropriate for your classroom
    ? Indicates interventions you need clarified or want to think about for a while
    T Indicates interventions for which you'd like more training
    X Indicates new interventions you plan to try soon

Strategy 1: Minimize the attention.

_____ Ignore the behavior.

_____ Give "The Eye."

_____ Stand close by.

_____ Mention the student's name while teaching.

_____ Send a secret signal.

_____ Give written notice.

_____ Give an I-message.

Strategy 2: Legitimize the behavior.

_____ Make a lesson out of the behavior.

_____ Extend the behavior to its most extreme form.

_____ Have the whole class join in the behavior

_____ Use a diminishing quota.

Strategy 3: Do the unexpected.

_____ Turn out the lights.

_____ Play a musical sound.

_____ Lower your voice.

_____ Change your voice.

_____ Talk to the wall.

_____ Use one-liners.

_____ Cease teaching temporarily.

Strategy 4: Distract the student.

_____ Ask a direct question.

_____ Ask a favor.

_____ Change the activity.

Strategy 5: Notice appropriate behavior.

_____ Thank students.

_____ Write well-behaved students' names on the chalkboard.

Strategy 6: Move the student.

_____ Change the student's seat.

_____ Send the student to the thinking chair.

3

SECTION THREE

Taking Corrective Action: Understanding Power and Revenge Behaviors

Power-seeking behavior is on the rise. Hundreds of teachers corroborate this fact. If present societal trends continue, we'll probably have to cope with more and more students who engage in power and revenge seeking. However, once we've stocked our toolbag with techniques for dealing with this behavior, we won't feel so frustrated and defeated.

Characteristics of Power Behavior

Power-seeking students constantly challenge us. Through words and actions, they try to prove that they are in charge, not us. Sometimes they stage a scene over major issues such as tardiness, incomplete work, or making noise while others are working. At other times they challenge us over relatively insignificant issues such as muttering under their breath when asked to do something or chewing gum in gym. They may completely disregard our instructions, or they may comply insolently with what we ask them to do.

Often power-seeking students don't act out until they're assured of an audience. We fear that if we lose such a public battle, we'll be labeled a "loser" by the entire class until school's out in June. The pressure of having to handle such a difficult situation with so much at stake in front of an audience adds greatly to our discomfort.

Power behaviors, like attention-seeking behaviors, display both active and passive modes. Let's consider the active mode first, since it's the easiest to notice.

Active Power Behavior

Temper Tantrums

Youngsters don't lose their temper; they use it. Young students, from preschool through the first couple of grades, may demonstrate temper by crying, kicking, rolling on the floor, and refusing to listen.

Did you ever know a child to go to his or her room, close the door, and then throw a tantrum? Or retire to the remotest corner of the playground before beginning to perform? Of course not. A temper tantrum is designed to manipulate an adult into submitting to a child's demands.

You can see instances of this at your local supermarket. Watch little Annabelle, cute as buttons in her new blue corduroys and matching shirt, screaming at the top of her lungs because Mommy has refused to buy her bubble gum. If you observe closely, you'll see that every few moments, Annabelle peeks out from her squeezed-shut eyes to make sure Mommy's hooked. If she's not, the little cutie repositions herself directly under Mommy's feet, turns up the volume, and proceeds with her tantrum!

Verbal Tantrums

Older students tend to throw verbal tantrums, often termed "lip" or "sass." They talk back to the teacher in a disrespectful and defiant manner: "You can't make me write out that chemistry experiment. Mr. Gunderman doesn't make his class do all that extra stuff, so I'm not going to do it either." Power-hungry students know more than a million variations of the you-can't-make-me-do-it theme.

One variation of verbal tantrums is the "lawyer syndrome." Students who use this behavior are bright and fluent. Instead of acting disrespectfully, they speak in a pleasant manner while using pseudologic to explain misbehavior: "There's no sense in my writing out that chemistry experiment because it takes away from the time I could better spend memorizing formulas. You saw me perform the experiment in class, so you already know that I can do it correctly."

The first time we lock horns with lawyer-syndrome students we might be impressed by their verbal acuity. Repeated encounters with these students wear us out, however, and we quickly become disenchanted with their linguistic acrobatics.

One variation on verbal tantrums is the "lawyer syndrome."

Passive Power Behavior

Quiet Noncompliance

Passive power seekers rarely cause a scene, because they've noticed that their classmates often get into double trouble for a single incident of misbehavior—once for not complying and once for spouting off at the mouth when confronted. Passive power seekers therefore avoid the pitched battle. Instead, they smile at us and say what we want to hear. Then they do precisely what they want to do. Mali's actions exemplify this behavior:

The writing assignment was passed out ten minutes ago, and Mali is still staring out the window, blank paper on her desk. When the teacher asks her if anything is wrong, Mali smiles and shakes her head. When asked why her paper is blank, she replies that she is thinking. When asked if she is going to complete the assignment, she nods affirmatively. At the end of the period, when the papers are collected, Mali's paper remains blank.

Mali has just defied the teacher as clearly as if she'd said, "I won't do it." She has done it in such a way, however, that the teacher may not recognize that a power struggle is occurring. The teacher becomes caught up in Mali's words, which sound compliant, and it takes a while for the teacher to realize that Mali's actions are a direct challenge to authority.

When we are faced with a similar situation, we should ascertain that our teaching methods and materials are appropriate for the student. We should also ensure that no learning disability or skill deficiencies could account for the student's actions. Once this has been done, we can be fairly certain that the motivation for such behavior is passive power.

Students seeking passive power exhibit sneaky behavior, for their words represent one thing and their actions another. Psychologists call this phenomenon "incongruent communication." When we receive such mixed messages from students, we tend to believe the words, not the behavior. So when a student says "I will" and then proves by subsequent actions "I won't," we keep hoping that somehow the "I will" is going to win out in the end. It won't—not until we respond differently.

Why do we tend to believe the words and not the behavior? Perhaps because we, as educators, tend to be verbal people. Words, after all, are our business. Moreover, we probably believe the words because we're idealistic and want to give students the benefit of the doubt: "If Mali says she'll do it, I keep hoping she will." Perhaps we believe the words because believing the behavior would demand corrective action, and we're not sure what action to take.

Labels Assigned to Passive Power Seekers

If we recall what psychologists have been maintaining for a long time—that it's far easier to lie with words than with behavior—then we'll quickly realize that the words of passive power seekers comprise a lie. When Mali says "I'm working on it" and then turns in a blank paper, she has, in effect, lied. But *lie* is a loaded word, with all kinds of unpleasant personal and ethical ramifications. Since calling anyone a liar, especially a young person, is risky, all kinds of euphemistic terms or labels are used to justify the discrepancy between what passive power seekers say they will do and what they actually do.

Unfortunately, these labels may interfere with our taking appropriate disciplinary action. The labels make what is really a bid for power seem instead to be some ingrained personality trait that the student couldn't possibly be expected to overcome. Such labels may be used to explain to parents and administrators why we're not having any success redirecting the student. Moreover, once we've labeled the student, we can more or less ignore the student and concentrate instead on coping with those engaged in more disruptive behavior.

The Lazy Label

Lucinda comes in on Monday morning without her weekend assignment. She smiles apologetically and says, "I'm sorry I didn't get it done. I really meant to do it, but I guess I'm just too lazy. I'll try to do better next time. Really!"

Lucinda's contriteness will usually win an extension from most teachers. After all, her good intentions should count for something. If she had told the truth instead—"I just didn't feel like doing homework this weekend"—she would have risked her teacher's wrath and might have faced unpleasant consequences.

When students hand me the "lazy" excuse, I ask them from whom they inherited their lazy genes. Mom? Dad? Grandpa Joe? I use humor to make the point that laziness isn't an inherited trait or a personality characteristic that cannot be changed. Laziness is a cover-up, an excuse for slacking off. Laziness is a chosen behavior, and once we have identified laziness as power behavior in operation, we can work to change it.

The Forgetful Label

"Oh, I forgot to do it!" is a phrase the average teacher hears thousands of times. Saying "I forgot" is more acceptable than saying "I refuse." No one has ever been expelled for forgetting!

Occasionally, the "forgetful" label is biologically appropriate, as when some neurological condition causes a student to forget things unintentionally. In addition, almost everyone experiences a memory lapse from time to time. The difference between these situations is that unintentional forgetting happens across the board—pleasant things as well as unpleasant things are forgotten. In contrast, power-behavior forgetting happens only when something unpleasant was supposed to have been done, such as chores or homework. The same student who invariably forgets her homework assignments can probably recite with ease which TV programs are broadcast on Monday night or the phone numbers of her five best friends.

The Short-Attention-Span Label

"Short attention span" is another label that a few young people neurologically merit and that a large number of them exploit. The exploiters find that exhibiting a short attention span is a convenient way to get teachers off their backs and reduce their workload. Take the case of first-grader Throckmorton Van der Camp. He just can't seem to concentrate on whatever the class is doing. His attention wanders, his body wanders, and his poor teacher has to wander after him. Yet during free time, he can sit in the block corner for hours, never moving his little bottom one inch. What a powerful manipulator!

As in the case of forgetting, if the student is selective with a short attention span, be suspicious. The problem is probably a "choosing disability" rather than a learning disability.

The Underachieving Label

A few years ago I counseled a student labeled "underachieving" by his teachers. Although he was gifted intellectually, his grades were poor and his work habits were nonexistent. Despite his unimpressive high school record, he used his charm to persuade a nearby state university to accept him.

During his first college vacation, he told me that he'd received an A in physics. When I asked if he'd been getting A's all along in physics, he said that he'd flunked the first three exams. When I expressed surprise that he'd been able to turn things around so well, he grinned and said, "It was easy. I just figured out that all I had to do was study."

My head spun with the thought of how many times over the past years this young man's teachers had begged and pleaded with him to study. This student's underachieving had been his way of exhibiting passive power all along; fortunately, he realized on his own that he had the ability to change his behavior.

Many times I've had students explain to me why they chose to do just so much work and no more in a specific class. In their own minds, they were reaching their goals precisely. This passive power behavior tells the teacher, "I'll decide exactly what level to achieve. You can't make that decision for me."

Students learn to exploit the "short-attention-span" label.

The Listening-Problems Label

Sometimes students who use passivity to gain power are labeled with "listening problems." If a student shows evidence of a real hearing problem, by all means have an audiologist run some tests. Most students with listening problems have problems with *doing*, however—not with hearing. They hear what we say perfectly well; they just choose not to respond.

Other Labels

Other labels used for passive power behaviors include *strong-willed, stubborn, unmotivated,* and *apathetic.* Of course, students who refuse to do work are stubborn, and students who won't follow rules are indeed strong-willed. No genetic basis exists for such behavior—though some parents will argue this point: "I know Constance is giving you trouble in class, but she's just like her father, the most stubborn man on earth. I guess you'll just have to live with it."

No, we don't have to live with it! Once we help students see that they do have the ability to change their behavior, we can influence them to make more appropriate choices.

Distinguishing Disabilities from Passive Power Behavior

Distinguishing a real learning disability from passive power behavior is not easy. As noted in the discussions on forgetfulness and short attention span, a key tip-off is selectivity. If the student fails to perform only when we ask him to do something but seems capable of completing tasks he has selected himself, we can be fairly sure that we're dealing with passive power behavior.

Some students may confuse us further by combining a small legitimate disability with a large chunk of power behavior. For example, consider Crawford, a ninth grader who has a slight auditory retention problem. If he looks directly at the teacher during lectures so that visual cues are combined with auditory cues, and if he takes copious notes, Crawford can retain most information. When he chooses not to do work, however, he consistently pleads, "I don't remember hearing that." Crawford's problem is not with listening but rather with doing; he uses his slight disability as a cover-up for choosing not to do what needs to be done.

Whenever we suspect that a student may have a disability, we need to work with the support staff to find out the exact nature of the problem. Once we know a student's capabilities, we can expect the student to live up to her potential, and we can treat any slacking off for what it is: passive power behavior.

Teacher and Student Response Clues

Teacher Response to Behavior

We can take two readings of our emotional gauge to help us identify whether the goal of a student's misbehavior is power. One reading concerns our feelings about the misbehavior. Power behavior usually incites strong feelings such as anger, frustration, or even fear. The second reading of our emotional gauge concerns our initial action impulse, or how we're tempted to immediately end the behavior before we stop to think. Initial action impulses for power behavior are inclined to be physical, such as an urge to shake the misbehaving student.

Student Response to Intervention

A further clue to identifying whether the goal is power concerns the student response when we try to end the misbehavior. When we intervene with students seeking power, we are often faced with a confrontational response. "You can't make me!" is the face-to-face challenge of power seekers, even though it may remain unspoken. Like the gunfighters in *High Noon,* they patiently wait to see what we'll do next. They usually continue the misbehavior until they're satisfied that they've "saved face"; that is, until they're sure that everyone present is convinced they've stopped the misbehavior on their own terms.

Origins of Power Behavior

Unfortunately, power-seeking behavior is on the rise. Hundreds of teachers corroborate this fact wherever I go. Teachers also are seeing more of this behavior among younger students than previously. Even preschools and kindergartens are increasingly filled with little bosses who only want to do things their way.

Changes in Relationships

The growth of power behavior in the classroom is a reflection of rapid changes occurring in the world around us. One hundred years ago, power relationships in our society were clearly defined. Dad ruled the household—and Mom expected to demur to him. Bosses ruled the workplace, and workers who challenged them lost their jobs. Teachers were governed by school boards that dictated everything from lifestyle to moral code.

Within this pecking order, children were at the bottom. They were to be seen and not heard, and any use of power tactics on their part led to severe punishment. In those days, when students could see the dominant-submissive relationship at work all around them, they accepted (but not necessarily liked) the "rule of the paddle."

Today all that has changed. No class or group of people accepts a subservient role. Everyone demands equality. Women demand equal rights, equal pay, equal responsibilities. Workers form unions, insisting on a voice in wage settlements and working conditions. Teachers, no longer willing to accept the "benevolent wisdom" of school boards, speak up about what they want, what they need, and what they will do.

The quest for personal power is pervasive. Young people notice this and want what they consider their fair piece of the action. In a society where almost no one models unconditional compliance with authority, we can't expect students to assume a subservient attitude. The only way to convince them to reaccept the rule of paddle power would be to provide them with suitable models of the dominant-subservient relationship. Women, workers, and even teachers would have to be persuaded to return to the roles of an earlier day.

I admit to having oversimplified a complex historical process, but the fact is that power relationships in society have been irrevocably altered. We can't turn back the clock; we can only move forward with the times. As teachers, we have to learn new strategies for coping with a relatively new and increasingly prevalent kind of classroom behavior.

The Human Potential Movement

The rise of power behavior has been hastened in the last few decades by a second factor: the trend toward personal growth and development. This trend is epitomized by the human potential movement that began in the late 1960s with the advent of humanistic schools of psychology. The focus of the movement is the exaltation of the individual and the gain of personal power. People attend workshops with themes such as "Unleashing Personal Power," and fill their bookshelves with best-selling titles such as *Born to Win* and *Pulling Your Own Strings*. For many, involvement in the movement is a positive experience.

Educators developed affective education in response to the personal growth trend, with their duty becoming not only to teach students the traditional three Rs but also to help them define their personal values, develop their individual talents, and enhance their social skills. For young people—as for the adults involved in the human potential movement—affective education is generally a positive experience.

Young people, however, sometimes confuse their yearning for personal power with a desire for interpersonal power. When this happens, they may overstep the bound and attempt to control not only themselves but also their teachers and classmates. As a result, teachers have to learn how to sidestep the power struggles and help students exercise legitimate personal power in ways that enhance the classroom atmosphere while satisfying student individuality.

Power Behavior's Silver Lining

Like attention-seeking behavior, power-seeking behavior has a silver lining. Many students who engage in this behavior—especially the active, verbal variety—exhibit desirable personal characteristics:

• leadership potential

• assertiveness

• independent thinking

These students will never be human doormats. By wanting to think for themselves and to control their own lives, they exhibit the signs of what represents good mental health in adults. The difficulty is that the students confuse personal power with interpersonal power and attempt to make decisions and exercise control inappropriately for their age and development.

Principles of Prevention

Students who engage us in a power confrontation may be imagined as dangling a rope in front of us. They are baiting us, daring us to grab one end of the rope so they can pull us into an embarrassing and frustrating tug-of-war. Since such students choose the time, place, and issue of the power struggle, we're bound to lose if we take the rope. We're better off if we let the rope dangle, untouched, and instead apply these principles of prevention:

• avoid and defuse direct confrontations (Chapter 9)

• grant students legitimate power (Chapter 16)

If present societal trends continue, we'll probably have to cope with more and more students who engage in power behavior. However, once we've stocked our toolbag with techniques for dealing with this type of behavior, we won't feel so frustrated and defeated. Having ready solutions to apply to the problems that we encounter will help us face each teaching day with confidence and composure.

Take Step 2: Identify the Goal of the Misbehavior

The goal of the student's misbehavior is entered under Step 2 of the School Action Plan. To determine whether the student employs power-seeking behavior, use the Chapter 7 Chart as a guide to assessing the behavior descriptions that you've listed under Step 1 of the plan. This chart summarizes the key information about power behavior that's presented in this chapter. Another chart that enables you to evaluate the characteristics of power behavior in conjunction with those of attention, revenge, and avoidance-of-failure behaviors is presented in Appendix A, Review Chart of the Four Goals of Misbehavior.

The teacher and student response clues are most helpful in deciding whether power is the goal of misbehavior. Take note of your feelings and your initial action impulse when the student misbehaves, and also how the student responds when you intervene to stop the behavior. The teacher and student response clues to each of the four goals of misbehavior are summarized in Appendix B, Teacher and Student Response Clues to Identifying the Goal of Misbehavior, a handy reference for double-checking identification of a particular goal.

Characteristics of Power Behavior

Active Power Behavior	*Temper tantrums and verbal tantrums:* Student is disruptive and confrontational.
Passive Power Behavior	*Quiet noncompliance:* Student does his or her own thing, yet often is pleasant and even agreeable.
Teacher Response to Behavior	*Feelings:* Anger, frustration, or fear. *Action impulse:* Physical.
Student Response to Intervention	*Response style:* Confrontational. *Response action:* Misbehavior continues until stopped on student's terms.
Origins of Behavior	Changes in society that stress equality in relationships, rather than dominant-submissive roles. The exaltation of the individual and the emphasis on achieving personal power, as epitomized by the human potential movement.
Silver Lining	Student exhibits leadership potential, assertiveness, and independent thinking.
Principles of Prevention	Avoid and defuse direct confrontations. Grant student legitimate power.

1   Give some examples of active and passive power behaviors that you've observed in your classroom.

_____

_____

_____

2   Do you agree with the suggested reasons why students engage in power behavior? Why or why not?

_____

_____

_____

3   The silver lining in power-seeking behavior is that students who seek power exhibit leadership potential, assertiveness, and independent thinking. Do you agree with this statement? Why or why not?

_____

_____

_____

4   Complete this sentence: When I was a child, one way I engaged my teachers or parents

in a power struggle was _____

_____

_____

_____

CHAPTER 8
Characteristics of Revenge Behavior

Young people who display attention-seeking or power behaviors can be delightful, charming students when not misbehaving. Not so students who habitually seek revenge. These students often sulk and scowl even when not lashing out. They put us on edge because they seem ready to explode at the slightest provocation. Their cumulative folders, full of adjectives such as *mean, vicious,* and *violent,* warn that trouble lies ahead.

When students misbehave to get revenge, they are retaliating for real or imagined hurts. Such behavior often follows power-seeking tactics, especially if the teacher has responded to the power behavior with a show of force. Although we are able to put students back in their place for a moment with a show of ultimate power, such a show is usually counterproductive, for it spawns worse misbehavior as students seek revenge. The misbehavior may come two minutes, two hours, two days, or two weeks after the original confrontation, but we can bet it's coming! Although we may win the battle by force, we'll lose the war by siege.

Not all revenge behavior results from a power struggle with a teacher. Sometimes the revenge seeker feels slighted by the teacher, even though the slight is unintentional. I encountered such a situation with Randy, one of my second graders. Randy frequently declared how much he disliked me, which hurt my feelings since I liked him and went out of my way to be nice to him. One day, he decided to attack me indirectly by knocking over a plant "accidentally-on-purpose." That was the last straw for me. "What have I done to make you dislike me so much?" I demanded.

His eyes full of hurt, Randy replied, "How come I never get to take the erasers outside? I guess you don't like me as much as the other kids." I was stunned by Randy's interpretation of events. I never dreamed that clapping the erasers outside was considered such a treat. I thought it was a great bore, and assigned it to students at random. Once I was able to understand things from Randy's perspective, I knew why he acted as he did, and was able to end the revenge attacks.

Revengeful students may not be angry with their teacher. They may have been hurt by parents, other teachers, administrators, or peers—people against whom revenge might be too risky. Their teacher then becomes a handy scapegoat, available five days a week. Teachers may also become ready targets when young people experience anger or hurt because of a distressing personal circumstance such as divorce, parental unemployment, or racial prejudice.

Active Revenge Behavior

Direct Physical Attacks

In keeping with the ever-increasing violence of the times, students frequently threaten teachers with bodily harm. From elbow jabs to knife slashings, violent student behavior is no longer merely a teacher's nightmare but rather a frighteningly real possibility.

Indirect Physical Attacks

Students get indirect physical revenge by breaking, damaging, or stealing something. Angry students may knock breakable items off our desk, snip buds off our plants, let air out of our tires, or take money from our wallet. Since students know we care about school property, they may break classroom windows, scratch desk tops, rip pages out of library books, or decorate lavatories with spray paint.

Psychological Attacks

Verbal Variety

Verbal psychological attacks frequently assume the form of threats, insults, or criticisms. Students who use this tactic know 1,001 ways to say "I hate you." Such psychological attacks rarely reflect the true quality of the teacher-student relationship; rather they are meant to manipulate the teacher into feeling hurt and guilty.

Youngsters always know which words will hurt adults the most. The mother of a preschooler came to me worried and upset, thinking her daughter was emotionally disturbed. When the girl became angry, she would say, "I hope a gorilla smashes your new car!" Was the child disturbed? No. Clever? Yes. No plain old "I hate you" for this verbal youngster. She had designed a unique threat to elicit maximum guilt from Mom—and she had succeeded.

Here are some of the most common varieties of psychological attack:

- You're the worst teacher I've had yet.
- My sister sure is lucky. She has a great teacher this year.
- I'm glad I don't really need to know this subject to get into college because you sure can't learn anything in this class.
- If this class were any more boring, they'd have to give out pillows with the textbooks.

Students who use the verbal variety of revenge know 1,001 ways
to say "I hate you."

Classroom teachers are not the only victims of psychological attacks. While conducting an inservice workshop for school librarians, I asked, "What variations of 'I hate you' do students use in the library?" These are some of the psychological attacks the librarians had experienced:

• There's nothing good to read in here.

• How come you don't have anything interesting for me?

• Who cares about dumb old books anyway?

If we remember that such negative statements are a form of revenge behavior, we won't get caught up in endless verbal battles, trying to convince students to change their minds.

Action Variety

Students usually know what values are held dear by teachers, and a favorite way to seek psychological revenge is to violate these values. For example, if we believe that cleanliness is second only to godliness, students who want to hurt us may muss their clothes before coming to class, keep their desks in disarray, or turn in sloppily done assignments. All our reprimands about sloppiness will fall on deaf ears as long as the students want to upset us. Similarly, if students know we believe that politeness is of great importance, they may decide to irk us by shoving other students in the hall or by using four-letter words in class. If we insist on punctuality, revengeful students may appear three minutes late to class and turn in all assignments one day late. In short, students frequently find the right button to push when they want to get a rise out of teachers.

Some extreme revenge actions may hurt students as much as or more than teachers and parents. Unfortunately, some students want revenge so badly that they are willing to hurt themselves to get it. Rebellious delinquency, pregnancy, and drug abuse are transgressions of adult values that almost always have negative consequences for students. Suicide, sad to say, is the ultimate form of revenge for a few severely discouraged youngsters.

Passive Revenge Behavior

Most revenge behaviors are active, not passive. The hurtful messages come through loud and clear. The only revenge behavior that could be classified as passive is withdrawal. Withdrawn students are sullen, uncommunicative, and remote. We reach out to them in every way we know, but they consistently turn away. Their lack of response is meant to hurt and frustrate us, and it does. After all, we're teachers—we want to help, and we take pride in being able to make contact with students. Students get their revenge: we dance rings around them trying unsuccessfully to elicit a response but end up feeling guilty, worn out, and wounded by constant rejection.

Teacher and Student Response Clues

Teacher Response to Behavior

We can take two readings of our emotional gauge to help us identify whether the goal of a student's misbehavior is revenge. One reading concerns our feelings about the misbehavior. When encountering revenge behavior, we feel devastation, dislike, and hurt in addition to the anger, frustration, and fear that we feel when dealing with power behavior. Being the target of someone else's hostility is highly unpleasant, so our feelings are quite strong.

The second reading of our emotional gauge concerns our initial action impulse, or how we're tempted to immediately end the behavior before we stop to think. Our first impulse when confronted with revenge behavior is either to strike back or to escape from the situation. This response is part of the "fight or flight" syndrome that has kept the human race alive from the beginning. Neither alternative is acceptable for teachers.

I learned this lesson the hard way. Once when I was observing a kindergarten class, a student crept up behind me and bit my arm. Instinctively, I bent down and bit him back. "You bit me!" he exclaimed, wide-eyed.

"You bit me," I responded.

He looked at me for a moment, then nodded and walked away. That ended the incident for him, but not for me. First I had to explain to the kindergarten teacher why I had bitten the student. Then I had to confess to the principal and fill out a number of official forms. The final and certainly most embarrassing step was calling the boy's parents to explain why a teacher had bitten their son.

We're all human. Our instinctive response when we're hurt is frequently to hurt back. Fortunately, we're able to suppress this initial impulse most of the time and use negotiation and conflict resolution skills instead.

Student Response to Intervention

An additional clue to identifying whether the goal is revenge concerns the student response when we try to end the misbehavior. When we intervene with students engaged in revenge behavior, they respond in a hurtful way. They take the confrontation one step further, adding to the showdown another dimension designed to offend us personally. The students will intensify the situation before they stop on their own terms. They not only try to maintain the appearance of being in control but also seek an additional way to hurt us.

Origins of Revenge Behavior

The increasing violence in schools is a reflection of the increasing violence in society. Everywhere, crime is growing in geometric proportion. TV screens are filled with acts of violence, and so are city streets, country roads, and suburban sidewalks. Rarely do youngsters see hurt feelings or anger expressed in positive ways; instead they constantly observe people lashing out at one another. It's not surprising, then, that their own feelings boil into similarly uncontrolled violence.

Revenge Behavior's Silver Lining

To see the silver lining in revenge behavior, we have to switch our perspective to that of the students. They see the hurting of another person as a means of protecting themselves from further hurt. They actually are showing a spark of life in their actions. For the sake of their own mental health, they're better off doing something than doing nothing. For example, a student who feels hurt but does nothing about it is likely to be overcome by feelings of hopelessness and despair. Such feelings, if they last long enough and are strong enough, can lead toward chronic depression and suicide. To know this is true, we have only to consider the sad statistics of young people who take their own lives. Suppressed feelings of pain are not the only cause of teenage suicide, of course, but they certainly constitute a major contributing factor.

Principles of Prevention

Two general principles are applicable for preventing or decreasing the amount of revenge behavior occurring in our classroom. The first is to build caring relationships with students who employ this behavior. Reassuring these students that we care about them despite their actions takes a great deal of courage and commitment. Resenting a person who wants to hurt us is natural; however, if we can manage to "separate the deed from the doer," as Chaim Ginott admonishes, we'll have a better chance of feeling a little bit positive about the student.[1] Chapter 11 suggests additional ways to form relationships with students whom we tend to dislike because of their disruptive and destructive behaviors.

The second principle of prevention involves teaching students how to express their hurt and hostility appropriately and inviting them to talk to us when they are upset. When students learn such skills, they learn how to resolve conflicts they feel by negotiating and communicating rather than by lashing out. Chapter 11 includes specific ways in which we can help students learn how to safely verbalize and vent their feelings.

Take Step 2: Identify the Goal of the Misbehavior

The goal of the student's misbehavior is entered under Step 2 of the School Action Plan. To determine whether the student employs revenge behavior, use the Chapter 8 Chart as a guide to assessing the behavior descriptions that you've listed under Step 1 of the plan. This chart summarizes the key information about revenge behavior that's presented in this chapter. Another chart that enables you to evaluate the characteristics of revenge behavior in conjunction with those of attention, power, and avoidance-of-failure behaviors is presented in Appendix A, Review Chart of the Four Goals of Misbehavior.

The teacher and student response clues are most helpful in deciding whether revenge is the goal of misbehavior. Take note of your feelings and your initial action impulse when the student misbehaves, and also how the student responds when you intervene to stop the behavior. The teacher and student response clues to each of the four goals of misbehavior are summarized in Appendix B, Teacher and Student Response Clues to Identifying the Goal of Misbehavior, a handy reference for double-checking identification of a particular goal.

Note

1. Chaim G. Ginott, *Teacher and Child: A Book for Parents and Teachers* (New York: Avon Books, 1972), 71.

Characteristics of Revenge Behavior

Active Revenge Behavior	*Physical and psychological attacks:* Student is hurtful to teacher, classmates, or both.
Passive Revenge Behavior	Student is sullen and withdrawn, refusing overtures of friendship.
Teacher Response to Behavior	*Feelings:* Dislike, hurt, devastation in addition to anger, frustration, fear. *Action impulse:* Fight or flight.
Student Response to Intervention	*Response style:* Hurtful. *Response action:* Misbehavior continues and intensifies until stopped on student's terms.
Origins of Behavior	A reflection of the increasing violence in society. Media role models that solve conflicts by force.
Silver Lining	Student shows a spark of life by trying to protect self from further hurt.
Principles of Prevention	Build a caring relationship with the student. Teach student how to express hurt and hostility appropriately and invite student to talk to us when she or he is upset.

1 Give some examples of active and passive revenge behaviors that you may have experienced.

_____

_____

_____

2 Do you agree with the suggested reasons why students engage in revenge behavior? Why or why not?

_____

_____

_____

3 The silver lining in revenge behavior is that students demonstrating such behavior show a spark of life by trying to protect themselves from further hurt. Do you agree with this statement? Why or why not?

_____

_____

_____

4 Complete this sentence: When I was a child, one way I attained (or fantasized attaining) revenge against my teachers or parents was _____

_____

_____

_____

CHAPTER 9
Avoiding and Defusing Confrontations

Six Guidelines for Intervention

This chapter presents guidelines that are most helpful in applying intervention strategies when the goal of the misbehavior is power or revenge, although many of the guidelines are also useful when the goal is attention or avoidance-of-failure. This is because the guidelines concern us: how we should behave when our students misbehave. By following the guidelines, we can shape our attitudes and actions to achieve the desired outcome of a teacher-student interaction. No matter how well we've matched an intervention to a misbehavior, we risk sabotaging success if our attitudes and actions are inappropriate.

Guideline 1: Focus on the Behavior, Not the Student

This guideline reemphasizes the concepts introduced in Chapter 4, which concerns writing accurate descriptions of a student's problem behavior. Just as we want to describe misbehavior objectively in our written records, so we want to act and speak objectively when we're intervening to stop a misbehavior. Dr. Chaim Ginott said it clearly: "Focus on the deed, not the doer; on the behavior, not the student."[1]

Describe behavior instead of evaluating it. When talking with students about their misbehavior, we need to use objective terms. If we concentrate on telling Tonye exactly what she is doing to cause us grief, we can avoid slipping in such subjective terms as *bad, wrong,* or *stupid.* Subjective terms provoke negative emotional reactions in the student (and in us) and get in the way of solutions.

Deal with the moment. When using an intervention technique, we need to deal only with what is happening at the moment. References to the past or to the future lock both the student and us into thinking that the misbehavior is part of an unalterable pattern. After all, if Alex "always" behaves in a certain way, and if we predict that he "always will," why should he try to behave differently?

Be firm and friendly. We need to be firm toward the misbehavior, thus making clear that it must stop. At the same time, we need to be friendly toward the student, thereby communicating our continuing interest and care. A firm but friendly[2] posture says to the student, "What you are doing must stop right now, but I still like you." This attitude of acceptance projects our belief that the student is capable of behavior that's appropriate. That belief can become a self-fulfilling prophecy.

Guideline 2: Take Charge of Negative Emotions

When a student misbehaves—particularly for power or revenge—our emotional response is immediately negative. We may feel angry, frustrated, fearful, or devastated. To feel such emotions is normal. After all, the student is disrupting our teaching process, stopping us from doing what we want or need to do.

Control negative emotions. When we allow anger to choke us or frustration to overwhelm us, we can't think clearly or act logically. Worse, if we display such negative emotions[3] to the student through body language or charged words, we may reinforce the student's decision to misbehave. For example, our anger is part of the desired payoff for students seeking power or revenge, so when we show them our anger, we're encouraging them to continue the misbehavior. A young student who can upset a grown-up is powerful indeed! High schoolers, too, enjoy a sense of power when they know they've succeeded in flustering a teacher.

When we manage not to act out our negative emotions, we do more than avoid reinforcing the misbehavior: we also set the stage for successful intervention. Dealing with misbehavior is like being forced to play a game. The student always starts the game by doing something unacceptable. Then the student expects us to make a predictable move—generally to react emotionally. The student's strategy is based on eliciting this anticipated reaction from us. When we take charge of our emotions and *respond* (rather than react predictably,) in a reasoned, noncombative manner, we check the student's strategy and thus communicate that we're unwilling to play the game. This gives us and the student the opportunity to become teammates who are trying to solve a mutual problem rather than opponents who are trying to outwit one another.

Release negative emotions. After we've responded to a misbehavior that's really upset us, we often have a lot of leftover negative feelings that need to be released. To get through the remainder of the teaching day without developing a headache or ulcers, we can promise ourselves that we'll get rid of the emotions as soon as we're in an environment where it's appropriate to do so. When we know relief is coming, we're usually able to contain our emotions for as long as necessary, without jeopardizing our interactions with students.

Many of us can find relief through physical outlets. For example, a brisk walk after school can help release negative emotions. The more athletic among us might find release through jogging, running, or a game of tennis. Those more practical might be surprised at how swiftly yardwork or housework can be accomplished when emotional energy is put into it!

My personal preference for releasing negative emotions is a verbal outlet. The audience is composed of me, and the environment is my car. On the way home from school, I keep the car windows closed, turn on the air-conditioning, heater, or radio so no other drivers can hear me, and pretend that the student I'm angry with is seated beside me. Then I let go with everything I'd like to say to the student.

If you want to try my method of releasing emotions, temporarily forget about the concepts that we've established for dealing with misbehavior. You don't have to focus on the behavior, be logical, or even maintain coherence. Just let it pour out, unrehearsed and unedited. Nothing you say can harm anyone. Be as loud as you want, and use whatever language you wish. I guarantee that by the time you reach your destination, you'll feel calmer than when you began the journey.

Guideline 3: Avoid Escalating the Situation

This recommendation goes hand in hand with the previous guideline. At the moment of misbehavior, we need to avoid certain behaviors that will only make the situation worse for both the student and us. To obtain a sampling of advice on what we should try to avoid doing or saying, I've surveyed scores of teachers, asking what specific behaviors have backfired for them. Here are some of their responses:

raising my voice	*making assumptions*
yelling	*backing the student into a corner*
saying "I'm the boss here"	*pleading or bribing*
insisting on having the last word	*bringing up unrelated events*
using tense body language, such as rigid posture and clenched hands	*generalizing about students by making remarks such as "All you kids are the same"*
using degrading, insulting, humiliating, or embarrassing put-downs	*making unsubstantiated accusations*
using sarcasm	*holding a grudge*
attacking the student's character	*nagging*
acting superior	*throwing a temper tantrum*
using physical force	*mimicking the student*
drawing unrelated persons into the conflict	*making comparisons with siblings, other students*
having a double standard—making students do what I say, not what I do	*commanding, demanding, dominating*
insisting that I am right	*rewarding the student*
preaching	

Some of these behaviors may stop a student from misbehaving—for the moment. But we'll pay too high a price for a short period of control; eventually, the negative side effects of our own behavior will give us more trouble than the student's original misbehavior.

All of the listed behaviors hinder students from feeling that essential sense of belonging. Most of the behaviors also reduce students' self-esteem. Some propel students into a more difficult interaction with the teacher, from attention-seeking

A young student who can cause a grown-up to become unglued is powerful indeed.

into power behavior or from power into revenge behavior. Why risk such negative side effects when we have the option of choosing more effective behaviors?

Were you surprised to discover *rewarding* on the list? Too often, any rewards that students receive encourage them to misbehave again in hopes of receiving more benefits. In addition, giving rewards promotes a bargaining mentality in some students. If we offer Tom a reward of ten minutes of extra free time if he will stop dawdling and finish his math worksheet, tomorrow he may ask, "If I finish this, do I get ten minutes of free time again?" If we say no, the worksheet probably will be completed s-l-o-w-l-y. If we say yes, we soon may hear this demand from Tom: "Teacher, I want fifteen minutes of free time for doing this math sheet." Before long, Theresa may ask, "If I finish, do I get extra free time too?" Soon our classroom will sound like "Let's Make a Deal," and we can forget about inspiring learning for its own sake.

Guideline 4: Discuss Misbehavior Later

There is a proper time for talking about misbehavior and negotiating solutions; however, that time is rarely at the moment of misbehavior. A brief, direct, firm, and friendly intervention is the best bet at the moment. Save the discussion for later.

Why not discuss misbehavior when it happens? Because neither the teacher nor the student will be able to hear one another's words since the moment is too emotional for both. This is particularly true of power and revenge confrontations, during which feelings run especially high.

The time to talk about the misbehavior is later—perhaps an hour later, perhaps tomorrow. When everyone has calmed down and can respond rationally, we can discuss the incident with the student. By then we'll be able to describe the misbehavior in ways that focus on the act, not the actor. We'll also be able to explain more clearly the effects and consequences of the misbehavior.

How will students know that their behavior is wrong if we don't tell them so at the moment? The answer to this legitimate concern is that most young people know what constitutes misbehavior and what the effects of that misbehavior will be. Consider Darryl, a seventh grader who shouts out four-letter words during health class. Does Darryl need to be told that his behavior is unacceptable? Not at all. In fact, we only increase Darryl's payoff for this misbehavior if we stop class to give Lecture 527 on the evils of profanity. Better to intervene immediately, saving the discussion for a time when Darryl's not getting the glory of it.

Students won't think we're condoning the misbehavior of their classmates if we hold general discussions about misbehavior from time to time. During these discussions, they'll learn what's acceptable and what's not. In addition, they'll learn that we will intervene quickly when someone misbehaves.

Guideline 5: Allow Students to Save Face

Students who seek power feel important only when they appear to be running the show. In their hearts, though, they know that the teacher has the ultimate authority and that they'll have to choose appropriate behavior eventually. As a result, they often do what we ask, but they do it their way—not ours. They try to play a game with us called "My Way." In this game, they give us what we want but stamp their compliance with a small gesture that says, "I'll do it—my way." If we play the game with them, we allow them to save face, and they give us what we want. Both players win.

A common ploy in the game of My Way is muttering. We ask Melinda to stop walking around the room and to return to her seat. She complies, but as she sits down, she mutters something under her breath. Her voice is not loud enough for us to understand what she's saying. Now what do we do? After all, she did sit down as we had requested.

If we decide that Melinda needs to sit down our way, not her way, the scene may proceed like this:

Teacher: Melinda, what did you say?

Melinda (very softly): Nothing.

Teacher: I heard you, Melinda. I want you to tell me what you said.

Melinda (in a loud, sarcastic voice): I was only thinking aloud to myself. Are you against thinking?

By insisting that students do things our way, we risk provoking a new confrontation, one that is often more unpleasant than the original. Is it worth it?

We also need to realize that a student's reaction to correction, such as muttering, is usually a normal human reaction—not a vindictive personal attack. For example, consider what the reaction might be in the following situation:

> *You're sitting in an emergency faculty meeting convened by your principal at 3:30 P.M. The principal has just distributed five inventory supply forms, saying that all the forms must be filled out immediately.*

Double standards do not help us build a cooperative spirit in the classroom.

What happens next? The room probably becomes filled with muttering, a perfectly human reaction when we're asked to do something we'd rather not do. Knowing that we must comply, we let off steam by muttering.

The game of My Way includes other tactics besides muttering. Students may take a few seconds longer to comply than is necessary or make a face or gesture that shows displeasure. They may repeat the forbidden action one last time before stopping or say something rude to have the last word. Allowing students to save face in these relatively harmless ways usually stops the misbehavior fairly quickly. Everyone's need has been satisfied: the teacher has achieved compliance, and the student has retained pride. Everybody wins!

Guideline 6: Model Nonaggressive Behavior

During a confrontation, everyone's emotions can get out of control easily. When this happens, people often communicate aggressively. Yelling, sarcasm, put-downs, rudeness, threats, insults, and humiliating remarks are examples of aggressive communication.

When caught in a revenge interaction, we're especially tempted to use aggressive tactics. To be effective, however, we need to use such tactics only in our imagination—not with our students.

No matter how well we learn to control our emotions and release them later, now and again our feelings may overcome us. When we are experiencing strong emotions and displaying aggressive behavior, we need to postpone taking any disciplinary action since we're likely to handle the situation poorly. Instead, we can use one of the graceful exit techniques as explained in Chapter 10, returning later to cope with the misbehaving student. Then, with our emotions under control, we'll be able to cope effectively with the problem.

Students learn how to communicate nonaggressively from us. They do what we do, talk like we talk. If we allow ourselves to become upset and act aggressively, they will too. By maintaining self-control, we invite students to do the same.

Notes

1. Chaim G. Ginott, *Teacher and Child: A Book for Parents and Teachers* (New York: Avon Books, 1972), 71.

2. This is a favorite aphorism of Dr. Rudolf Dreikurs.

3. Technically speaking, emotions are neither "negative" nor "positive." They are what they are. In popular usage, however, the feelings discussed—anger, hurt, frustration, hopelessness—are generally considered to be negative. So for ease and clarity of communication, I'll occasionally refer to "negative emotions."

Avoiding and Defusing Confrontations

Below are the recommended guidelines for applying intervention strategies, particularly when the goal of misbehavior is power or revenge. On the continuum under each guideline, mark where you think you are now in your ability to follow that guideline.

Guideline 1: Focus on the Behavior, Not the Student

I focus on the student.   I focus on the behavior.

←——→

Guideline 2: Take Charge of Negative Emotions

I display negative emotions.   I don't display negative emotions.

←——→

Guideline 3: Avoid Escalating the Situation

I often do or say things that   I avoid doing or saying things
make the situation worse.   that make the situation worse.

←——→

Guideline 4: Discuss Misbehavior Later

I discuss misbehavior when it occurs.   I discuss misbehavior later.

←——→

Guideline 5: Allow Students to Save Face

I don't allow students to save face.   I allow students to save face.

←——→

Guideline 6: Model Nonaggressive Behavior

I often act aggressively.   I never act aggressively.

←——→

4

Taking Corrective Action: Interventions for Power and Revenge Behaviors

Revenge behavior probably provokes the most difficult kind of teacher-student interaction. Since revenge behavior is not only disruptive but also destructive, our intense personal response to the misbehaving student may get in the way of effective action. But, though we may not be able to *like* revengeful students, we *can* learn strategies to help us coexist peacefully with them. The results will be well worth our efforts.

CHAPTER 10

When the Goal Is Power or Revenge: Interventions

No aspect of discipline is more difficult than dealing with power and revenge behaviors. The confrontations and disruptions that accompany them exhaust our energy, waste valuable teaching time, and dissipate our dedication to teaching.

Power and revenge behaviors can be compared to the eruption of a volcano. A volcano begins with the rumbling stage, during which the earth shakes and steam begins to spout forth. Next comes the mighty explosion, which destroys everything in its path. Eventually the resolution stage is reached, in which we cope with the damage and take steps to prevent further destruction.

Power and revenge confrontations parallel these volcanic stages. They, too, begin at the rumbling stage, with students using annoying antics to tempt us into a confrontation. Once we're hooked, the explosion comes—unpleasant words and behaviors spurt forth. Eventually, we reach the resolution stage, when we try to get everyone back to normal and prevent future confrontations.

Three Stages of a Classroom Volcano

This chapter presents intervention techniques for dealing with each stage of a classroom volcano. The techniques are grouped under three general strategies that parallel the stages:

- the rumbling stage: make a graceful exit
- the eruption stage: use time-out
- the resolution stage: set the consequences

If a graceful exit technique is successful at the rumbling stage, the eruption stage may be avoided. But despite our best efforts and no matter how polished our skills, the confrontation might reach the eruption stage. When this happens, we use a time-out technique, which enables both us and the student to calm down before entering the resolution stage. At the resolution stage, we implement consequences. This is also the time to educate the student to make more appropriate choices in the future.

The Rumbling Stage: Make a Graceful Exit

At the rumbling stage, we're warned that a full-scale confrontation is coming. We might see the warning in the students' facial expressions or body language, or hear it in their voices. We might sense it when they smile and disregard our instructions or when they ignore school rules. The warning gives us a chance to smother the confrontation by using a graceful exit technique.

A graceful exit technique is a diplomatic maneuver that allows all involved to save face. No one emerges as a winner or a loser; everyone is given the opportunity to step away from a heated situation.

When making a graceful exit, we need to remain as calm as possible. Any sarcasm in our voice or show of animosity in our actions will provoke further challenges from the students. The more humor we can bring to the situation, the more graceful the exit for everyone concerned.

Acknowledge Students' Power

That teachers have the power to *make* students do things is an illusion. For example, suppose Dawn refuses to do her math assignments. We can threaten and cajole, take away rights and privileges, and send notes home until we're blue in the face. But if Dawn doesn't *choose* to do the work, it won't get done. The more we try to control the student, the more the student resists.

Instead of fighting this losing battle, we can acknowledge the student's power: "Dawn, I can't make you do the math work." When we give up our control and command, the student has nothing to resist. Does this mean that we relinquish all authority and students like Dawn get to do whatever they want? Absolutely not. Once the student's resistance has been lowered and the confrontation calmed, we can use a consequence to influence Dawn to choose appropriate behavior.

Acknowledging the student's power quiets the situation because it is an admission of the student's equal status as a human being. People who feel dominated often react by resisting the person in charge. When we acknowledge that we can't dominate and that no one in the classroom is superior or inferior, we gain cooperation from students rather than confrontation.

Remove the Audience

Dr. Oscar Christensen of the University of Arizona loves to tell this story about a power interaction:

> *The two tall gladiators were having a real go of it in front of a crowd of students gathered outside the lunchroom. I walked up, told them to stop immediately, and was totally ignored. So then I said, "Anyone caught standing in this hall in one minute will be put on detention." The crowd dispersed immediately. A minute later, the gladiators noticed that their audience had deserted them, and stopped dead in their tracks. At that point I was able to remove the gladiators to my office to settle the matter between them in a more peaceful manner.*

When others are standing by to see who wins, confrontations invariably intensify. Sending the audience away is not always possible, especially when the confrontation happens in the classroom. We can sometimes postpone a classroom

73

Agreeing can be an excellent fogging technique.

confrontation until the period has ended and the rest of the students have gone. For example, we might suggest, "Carter, we'll finish discussing this matter as soon as the bell rings." Once class is over and Carter is without an audience, he may lose interest in a confrontation. Performances usually are pointless without spectators to applaud.

Table the Matter

It's the last class of the day, and we're weary to the bone. Hannah chooses this moment to challenge us by telling her friend—and the class at large—just how stupid last night's assignment was in her opinion. All eyes are on us, waiting to see what we'll do next. If we tangle with Hannah, the whole class is likely to get out of control, and we'll probably end up with a first-class headache.

Our best way out of such situations is to table further discussion by using a simple sentence or two that postpones resolution of the issue until we're better able to cope. We can choose our own time and place to continue the discussion, when the audience is gone and we're less emotional. Here are some examples of statements that can effectively table discussion:

- I'm not willing to talk with you about this right now.
- Would you rather fight or solve this problem? (If the student chooses "fight," we reply, "But not with me. Who would you like to fight about it with? The principal? Your parents?")
- You must be confusing me with someone else. I don't argue with my students.
- You may be right. Let's talk about it later.

Make a Date

Keep a datebook handy. When a student begins to challenge you, pick up the book and note a mutually selected time and place for a private conversation. Say nothing more at this point; simply continue with the lesson.

Use a Fogging Technique

When students attack us verbally, our best strategy is to use a fogging technique, which involves responding to inflammatory statements as if they are of little or no importance. Such a response tells students that we cannot be manipulated by their insults. The two most effective fogging techniques are to agree with the student and to change the subject.

Fogging techniques may seem contradictory to the skill of "active listening," which acknowledges the importance of what students are saying. When students are verbally attacking us, however, active listening will only prolong the confrontation. If the misbehaving students really wanted to discuss something, they'd bring up the matter at a more appropriate time and place. We can use the datebook technique to set a time to listen actively to the students' feelings if we think this is necessary.

Agree with the student. When students make insulting statements, the last response they expect from us is agreement. When we agree, students have no way to continue the confrontation.

Suppose Lewis sneeringly informs Ms. Hickory that she's by far the worst teacher on the planet. Ms. Hickory can simply respond, "You may be right. Now open your book to page fifty-seven." If Lewis continues to insult Ms. Hickory, she can continue to agree cheerfully while calmly reminding him which page the class is working on. After a short time, Lewis will realize that he does not have the power to engage Ms. Hickory in a confrontation that she does not choose to join, and he will drop his challenge.

Change the subject. If we reply to verbal attacks by changing the subject, we can deflate the student's challenge. For example, Ms. Hickory might respond to Lewis's insult by asking him if he watched the football game last night. If his attack continues, she can respond with a comment on the weather or tell a joke. Like a broken record, she can repeat her lines over and over again until Lewis gets the message that she's not going to fight.

We aren't condoning a student's words when we don't reply directly to his attack. He knows that his words are inappropriate and hurtful. A lecture on "Why Students Should Respect Teachers" won't help either; it will only prolong the confrontation. Our goal is to get the student to end his misbehavior, and if we can accomplish this quickly through fogging, we aren't required to do anything else at the moment.

The Eruption Stage: Use Time-Out

If a confrontation can't be contained during the rumbling stage, look out! The explosion is coming! Once we've entered the eruption stage, we'd be wise to get out of the way—fast. The various time-out techniques can help us do just that. Time-out involves isolating the student from the rest of the class. The frequency and seriousness of the misbehavior determines where we send the student. The time-out techniques are presented here in order of increasing severity.

Occasionally, revenge encounters bypass the rumbling stage and begin with the eruption. This can occur if the student has been upset by something that happened elsewhere—at home, in another classroom, on the playground. Once the explosion happens, we have to deal with the here and now, and can't worry about where and why the behavior originated.

Time-Out in the Classroom

A time-out area for young children in a self-contained classroom should be out of the direct line of vision of the rest of the students. One way to create such a space is to partition off a small area of the room with a piano, bookcase, or a movable chalkboard or bulletin board. We could also isolate the child by putting side partitions on a standard student desk or by using a carrel.

Time-Out in Another Classroom

An effective time-out area could be another classroom of the same grade. The students in another classroom usually aren't interested in being an audience for someone they don't really know, so they probably will ignore the misbehaving student. When the payoff of peer attention is removed, the student is less likely to continue the misbehavior.

I don't recommend sending a student to a classroom of younger children, since this move will likely embarrass or humiliate the student. A child whose self-esteem is thus lowered is not likely to be convinced to choose appropriate behavior. However, sending a student to a class of older children to experience how "mature" students behave is acceptable.

Time-Out in a Special Room

As a step between another classroom and the principal's office, some schools set up a supervised time-out area, detention room, or in-school suspension area to isolate misbehaving students from classmates.

Time-Out in the Office

The principal's office should be used only as a last resort. Sitting on a chair while phones ring and teachers buzz by is much too rewarding for some students. Besides, why advertise that our student has gotten so out of hand? Despite these disadvantages, we may have to make use of the office when all other in-school choices have failed or the misbehavior is so malicious that intermediate steps are out of the question.

Time-Out in the Home

The most severe time-out technique is suspension from school. This step should be avoided whenever possible since often no adult is home during the day to supervise a student who has been suspended. As a result, the student could get into additional trouble. Moreover, many young people consider staying out of school to be a reward, not a punishment. This is especially true if the household has all the attractions of a video arcade.

Enforcing Time-Out

The way to cope with stubborn students who refuse to go to a time-out area is to use these techniques: "language of choice" and the "Who Squad."

The language of choice. When we tell confrontational students what they "must do right now," we are asking for further resistance. Giving them a choice is more effective: "Bonita, you may sit quietly in your seat without heckling your classmates, or you may go to time-out in Mr. Jordan's room. You decide."

If Bonita verbally agrees to behave appropriately but continues to misbehave, the teacher can say, "I see by your behavior that you have chosen to go to Mr. Jordan's room. Please go now." No second chances. It's time for action, not words.

The language of choice usually defuses confrontations because we are not commanding, demanding, or threatening. We simply state the specific behavior expected and the consequence of noncompliance. We don't make students go to time-out; they make themselves go by choosing to continue to misbehave. Having the choice gives students a feeling of control, which makes them more likely to choose appropriate behavior. The only time the language of choice is useless is when the misbehavior is so disruptive or potentially dangerous that the students must be removed from the room immediately.

The Who Squad. Sooner or later, every teacher faces a student who is 100 percent recalcitrant. "You can't make me go to time-out," says the all-star quarterback to his five-foot teacher. At this point, the teacher can give a second choice: "Would you like to go by yourself, or would you like me to get someone who will help you go?" If the student continues to refuse to budge, it's time to call in the Who Squad.

Every school should designate pairs of staff members as the Who Squad, suggest Dubelle and Hoffman in their book *Misbehavin'*.[1] Anyone strong and willing can serve on this squad—administrators, counselors, teachers, custodians. The squad can be rotated depending on people's schedules.

When called for by a teacher, the Who Squad walks into the classroom and asks, "Who?" The teacher indicates the student, and the Who Squad whisks him or her away. Once students know that they can't get away with outright defiance, few of them will bother trying it.

The Who Squad should be called for immediately whenever a teacher feels physically threatened by a student. This is not a time for graceful exits or negotiation. Safety comes first.

Setting the Duration for Time-Out

The idea behind time-out is not to isolate students for hours on end, but rather to have them experience a few uncomfortable moments. Young students or first offenders can be given five minutes, while older students or repeat offenders might merit fifteen to thirty minutes. An alternative to setting the duration ourselves is to tell the student to return when she or he is ready to behave appropriately.

If misbehavior is resumed following a time-out, the next time-out should be increased in length, without student options for setting the limit. If the student still continues to misbehave, try another location and use consequences in addition to time-out.

Some teachers require a student to do schoolwork while in a time-out area; others prefer that the student sit and do nothing. If the time-out is to be longer than five minutes, keeping the student occupied is probably best. An idle mind and hands may find new ways to get into trouble.

The Resolution Stage: Set the Consequences

In the physical world, every action has an automatic reaction. Turn over a glass of milk (action) and out spills the milk (reaction). Put your hand on a hot stove and you get burned. Push the horn and it honks. Since students are familiar with learning through natural action-reaction sequences, misbehaviors (actions) can be paired with unpleasant consequences (reactions) so that students can learn from experience.

The sequence of action and reaction in the classroom isn't quite as automatic as it is in nature, however. Usually we have to arrange for the appropriate consequence to occur.

Establishing Consequences

We alone can determine consequences for a particular misbehavior, or we can ask students for suggestions. When students are involved in the decision-making process, they'll cooperate more readily, and since they know best what works for them, the consequences they help devise will probably be effective.

All students should know ahead of time what behaviors are expected and what consequences will occur if they choose to violate rules or limits. Once consequences have been established, the students should be allowed to experience the action-reaction sequence without interference. The goal is for students to learn from this arranged flow of events to choose more appropriate behavior in the future.

Presenting Consequences

A consequence is presented most effectively as a "when-then" statement: "*When* you do this (specific misbehavior), *then* this (specific consequence) will happen." "When-then" works better than "if-then." Students often tend to consider "if-then" statements empty threats that won't be carried through.

Guidelines for Effective Consequences

An effective consequence is "related, reasonable, and respectful," as noted by Jane Nelsen in *Positive Discipline*.[2] Explanations of these "three Rs" follow.

Related consequence. A related consequence is logically connected to the misbehavior. The more closely related the consequence and misbehavior, the more valuable the experience for the student. If Betsy continuously tips back her chair (misbehavior), she can be asked to stand for the rest of the period (consequence). This is what Betsy learns: "When I tip my chair back, I lose the privilege of sitting in it." A consequence of missing recess or staying after school would not be logically related to Betsy's misbehavior.

To maintain an appropriate relationship between the action and the consequence, we must establish consequences that take place at school, not at home. Some teachers get upset when I say this because they like parents to get involved in the discipline process. But enforcing consequences for school misbehavior is not a parental responsibility. Imagine how we'd respond if parents called on us to enforce consequences for misbehaviors that occurred at home: "Miss Detweiler, my daughter failed to make her bed this morning. Would you please take away her playground privileges as a consequence?"

When your back is against the wall, it's nice to know there's a "Who Squad" to call on.

Reasonable consequence. A reasonable consequence is equal in proportion and intensity to the misbehavior. We use consequences to teach students to behave appropriately, not to make them suffer. For example, suppose Cassandra has scribbled her name on a lavatory door. A reasonable consequence would be to have her scrub that door. An unreasonable consequence would be to have her scrub every door in the washroom. Although the latter would be an unforgettable lesson, the increase in her hostility level would not be worth it. We want to create a cooperative student, not a lifelong enemy.

Respectful consequence. A respectful consequence is stated and carried out in a way that preserves a student's self-esteem and doesn't discourage the student from being able to belong through positive behavior. It contains no name-calling, blaming, shaming, or implied moral judgment. It is not accompanied by lectures or discussions about behavior. Rather, the consequence is stated in polite, unemotional, matter-of-fact terms.

Consequences Versus Punishments

When consequences aren't related, reasonable, and respectful, they turn into punishments. Consequences and punishments are alike in that both take advantage of the action-reaction sequence: "When you do this, then this will happen." But punishments are not related to the misbehavior—instead, they are arbitrary. Punishments are not reasonable—instead, they are inequitable. Punishments are not respectful—instead, they are punitive. Punishment provokes hostility and antagonism in students, making cooperative discipline impossible.

Educator Jane Nelsen has another set of Rs to describe the results of using punishments rather than consequences:[3]

- Resentment (This is unfair. I can't trust adults.)
- Revenge (They are winning now, but I'll get even.)
- Retreat (I'm getting away from here.)
- Rebellion (I won't get caught next time.)
- Reduced self-esteem (I'm a bad person.)

Why risk the negative effects of punishments when we can use consequences to attain positive effects?

Choosing the Consequence

Jerrold Gilbert has performed a valuable service by classifying consequences into some helpful categories:[4]

Loss or delay of privileges

- of activity
- of using objects or equipment
- of access to areas in the school

Loss of freedom of interaction

- denied interactions with other students
- required interactions with school personnel
- required interactions with parents
- required interactions with police

Restitution

- repair of objects
- replacement of objects

Loss or delay of activity. When students misuse time through tardiness, dawdling, or disruption, we can ask that they "pay back" the squandered time; this can be done when we deny or delay an activity they enjoy such as free time, recess, or a field trip. Students also could be required to come to school before class or to stay after school as a consequence. The payback can be proportionate to the amount of time misused, and increased each time the same or a similar behavior occurs.

Keeping students from going to special classes such as gym, music, art, or shop is not a reasonable consequence. Special classes should not be considered subjects of lesser importance that can be withheld because of misbehavior elsewhere.

Loss or delay of using objects or equipment. Students who misuse books, laboratory apparatus, audiovisual equipment, sporting goods, or objects from home can be deprived of their use for a limited time.

Loss or delay of access to school areas. When students misbehave in certain areas, such as the lunchroom or library, these can become off-limits to them for a reasonable amount of time.

Denied interactions with other students. A student misbehaving for the sake of the audience can be denied interactions with peers for a short period of time. The time-out strategies already discussed are most effective for this purpose.

Required interactions with school personnel. When we are at an impasse with a student, we may want to require a meeting with the principal, guidance counselor, or the dean of students. The purpose is to talk about what's happened and to come up with a plan so that it doesn't happen again.

Required interactions with parents. Some misbehaviors require an interaction with parents. This was the case with Duane, a third grader who destroyed a classmate's art project. I called his mother, and asked Duane to please tell her what he had done. I didn't ask Duane's mom to apply consequences at home for this in-school problem. Rather, the phone call was simply to inform her that the misbehavior had occurred. Later in the book we'll learn how to involve parents and students in setting other consequences for the student.

Required interactions with police. Sometimes confrontational students break the law, perhaps through vandalism, stealing, or drug dealing. We should not shield these students from the legal consequences of their actions, for that only teaches them to "beat the system."

When we call in the police, we still have an obligation to help the young offenders choose appropriate behavior in the future. We'll want to use encouragement strategies to raise their self-esteem and to help them relate in positive ways to teachers and classmates. We'll also want to ask school support services—counselors, psychologists, and social workers—to work with the students and their families.

Restitution. When students lash out by stealing, damaging, or destroying something that belongs to us or to the school, we can intervene by insisting on restitution. We can require students to return, repair, or replace that which has been unreasonably taken, damaged, lost, or used up.

Repair of objects. Students can make restitution for physical damage to school property by performing a service that undoes the damage to the greatest extent possible. For example, students who scratch desks can sand and refinish them. Those who stuff toilets can mop floors. We may have to spend extra time supervising this work, but it's worth taking the time to teach responsibility.

Replacement of objects. Sometimes students slash tires, crack windows, rip library books, or break audiovisual equipment. Should students have to pay for the damage? Yes, if the money really comes out of their own pocket. No, if their parents foot the bill. When the latter happens, students learn that they can cause as much trouble as they like, and their folks will fix it up in the end. If students have no money of their own to pay for damage, they can contribute time doing janitorial or clerical services at school. The wages normally paid for such work can be used to pay for the damage. Again, the extra supervision needed will be worth it in the end.

Student Response to Consequences

Many students with power and revenge behaviors respond to consequences by putting on a show of nonchalance to preserve their pride in front of peers and to keep us from seeing that we've reached them. They hope this "I don't care" attitude will persuade us to remove the consequences. Don't be fooled by this mask of indifference. Truly appropriate consequences will have a beneficial effect on students whether they let on or not.

Take Step 3: Choose Intervention Techniques

If you've determined that the student who's the subject of your School Action Plan has power as his or her goal, select several of the intervention techniques described in this chapter and listed in the Chapter 10 Chart. If revenge is the goal, you'll want to select intervention techniques as well as read Chapter 11, which presents additional information about revenge behavior. Make your intervention choices on the basis of these factors:

- the student's age
- what makes the most sense to you
- what fits your teaching style and personality

Record the selected techniques under Step 3 of the plan.

As you complete this step, keep in mind that intervention does not mean punishment. Instead, think of intervention as guidance with a double purpose: to stop the behavior occurring at the moment and to influence the student to choose more appropriate behavior in the future.

A summary chart that includes interventions recommended for each of the four goals of misbehavior is presented in Appendix C, Summary Chart of Interventions.

Notes

1. Stanley Dubelle, Jr., and Carol Hoffman, *Misbehavin': Solving the Disciplinary Puzzle for Educators* (Lancaster, Pa.: Technomic Publishing Co., 1984), 49.

2. Jane Nelsen, *Positive Discipline* (Fair Oaks, Calif.: Sunrise Press, 1981), 67. Also available in an edition by Ballantine Books.

3. Nelsen, 23.

4. Jerrold Gilbert, "Logical Consequences: A New Classification," *Journal of Individual Psychology* 42 (no. 2): 243. The original categories relate to consequences at home, and they have been adapted somewhat to apply more directly to school situations.

Interventions for Power and Revenge Behaviors

General Strategy	Techniques

Make a graceful exit.	Acknowledge students' power.
	Remove the audience.
	Table the matter.
	Make a date.
	Use a fogging technique:
	  Agree with the student.
	  Change the subject.

Use time-out.	Time-out in the classroom. Time-out in another classroom. Time-out in a special room. Time-out in the office. Time-out in the home.

Set the consequences.	Loss or delay of activity.
	Loss or delay of using objects or equipment.
	Loss or delay of access to school areas.
	Denied interactions with other students.
	Required interactions with school personnel.
	Required interactions with parents.
	Required interactions with police.
	Restitution:
	  Repair of objects.
	  Replacement of objects.

CHAPTER 11
More About Revenge Behavior

Revenge behavior probably provokes the most difficult kind of teacher-student interaction. Since revenge behavior is not only disruptive but also destructive, our intense personal response to the misbehaving student may get in the way of effective action. We may even get to the point where we simply can't stand the student, and, as a result, we may be unable to apply discipline techniques with the necessary impartiality.

Forming Relationships with Students We Dislike

We may not be able to like revengeful students, but we can learn to coexist peacefully with them. They have the right to be treated with dignity and respect. The following strategies will help us do that. They'll take some time and effort to carry out, but the results will be worth it. Otherwise, we'll have difficulty intervening successfully when revengeful students misbehave and encouraging effectively when they behave appropriately. The changes start with us, the professionals, not with the students.

Change Our Perceptions

Finding the good in revengeful students is like panning for gold—we may have to sift through pail after pail of muck to find the sparkle. One shortcut to gaining the gold is to begin perceiving weaknesses as strengths. The key to this is using positive language in place of negative words. For example, we may think of Sebastian as "stubborn" until we check a thesaurus and find such positive synonyms as "steadfast," "resolute," and "persistent." If we start thinking of Sebastian's behavior in these terms, our perceptions can change for the better. We even might begin thinking of Sebastian as a regular Rock of Gibraltar!

Using positive language can help us interact more effectively with revengeful students. Suppose we ask Dorinda to stop tapping her pencil, and she substitutes her pen. When we put a stop to this, she uses her ruler. Then her fingers. At this point, we could get angry at Dorinda's deviousness. Or we could say, "Your creativity is too much for me. I can't possibly think of everything. Would you help me out and not tap anything?" Once Dorinda's behavior is given a positive label, she can stop misbehaving without losing face.

Teachers need physical outlets too.

Change Our Reactions

In Chapter 15, we'll learn about the five A's of encouragement: acceptance, attention, appreciation, affirmation, and affection. I can hear the howls now: "How can I possibly shower students I dislike with any of those A's?"

The task may be like taking bitter medicine at first, but if we can manage to swallow our dislike while we use encouragement strategies a few times a day for about a week or two, the relationship between us and the students is likely to change for the better. The students will perceive us differently, feel a greater sense of belonging, and probably respond more positively toward us. In turn, we'll feel more positive toward them.

Act Confident in Our Ability

Just as dogs attack when they sense fear, so will revenge-seeking students take advantage of any perceived weakness in us. We need to appear confident. If we don't feel confident, we can at least act that way, pretending that we can handle confrontations with relative ease. If we do this consistently, we may even start to feel confident.

Demonstrate That We Care

As Dubelle and Hoffman point out in *Misbehavin'*, our students don't need our love, but rather our care. We can't love them all, but we can show them all that we care what happens to them.[1] Caring is an action, not a feeling; it's something we do on behalf of the students. We can control our actions, even if our feelings are contrary. We can show our caring by taking steps to help revengeful students connect, contribute, and feel capable. These three Cs of encouragement are discussed in Chapter 2 of this handbook.

Teaching Students to Deal with Their Emotions

Revenge-seeking students can be greatly helped if they are taught how to safely vent their intense emotions. They will then have less need to lash out in hostility.

Verbalizing Feelings

During revenge interactions, we can ask students to tell us what they are feeling. If they're unwilling to answer directly, we can take a guess: "Looks to me like you're feeling upset and angry today. Are you?" If our guess is wrong, students usually will correct us. If they admit we're right, we can ask them to tell us more about their feelings.

When we're caught in a situation in which an immediate discussion about feelings would be inappropriate, we can acknowledge the student's emotions and set a time to talk later. It's often helpful to ask students to write down or tape-record how they feel at the moment, and then use that information as a starting point for the subsequent discussion.

When we talk with students about emotions, our job is simply to listen and to indicate that we hear what they are saying. We want to avoid telling students what they should or shouldn't feel or labeling their feelings as good or bad. Listening without responding with advice or judgments is hard. But as one former student pointed out to me, "You have two ears and only one mouth. That means you should listen twice as much as you talk."

After students have let out their feelings, we can ask, "What brings on these feelings?" If we're feeling brave, we can ask, "Is there anything I do that makes you feel that way?" When students are willing to talk about what we do that they find upsetting, we can learn a lot about our style of teaching and relating. If we think their comments are valid, we can make changes. If not, we needn't change a

We can change our perceptions of students we dislike.

thing. We don't need to discuss the validity of the comments with the students. All we need do is thank them for being so candid and say that we'll think about what they've said.

Physically Venting Feelings

Some students benefit from having a physical outlet for emotions. In a self-contained classroom for young children, an emotional-release corner can be set up in the back of the room. There, students can let out their feelings, perhaps by pounding clay. Older students need a separate space in the school building where they can go to safely vent strong feelings. Sometimes a counselor, gym teacher, or even a principal will maintain such a space. For example, a punching bag in the gym can be a well-used emotional outlet.

Applying Intervention Techniques

When students attack us with hurtful deeds rather than words, we can use the same intervention techniques that we use during power confrontations. Revengeful students are likely to be a bit more recalcitrant and will probably take more time to deal with than power-seeking students, however.

When using time-out as an intervention for revenge behavior, send the student to a designated place outside of the classroom. Separation from the teacher and the classroom gives the student a necessary cooling-off period. Make sure a Who Squad is available in case the student refuses to budge.

When using consequences as an intervention, be sure to follow the three Rs discussed in Chapter 10: make the consequences related, reasonable, and respectful. Revengeful students always have their antennae up, just waiting for us to do something to justify their lashing out again.

Note

1. Stanley Dubelle, Jr., and Carol Hoffman, *Misbehavin': Solving the Disciplinary Puzzle for Educators* (Lancaster, Pa.: Technomic Publishing Co., 1984), 53.

5

SECTION FIVE

Taking Corrective Action: Avoidance-of-Failure Behavior

We may fail to recognize avoidance-of-failure as a goal of misbehavior, since students who are avoiding failure generally do not distract us or disrupt our classroom. These students tend to observe school rules and requirements. The problem is that they seldom interact with teachers and peers. They usually remain isolated in the classroom, in the halls, and in the lunchroom. Often, students who fear failure simply don't do their schoolwork, quietly hoping we won't notice.

Characteristics of Avoidance-of-Failure Behavior

We may fail to recognize avoidance-of-failure as a goal of misbehavior, since the student who is avoiding failure generally does not distract us or disrupt our classroom. For example, consider Alphonse, slumped in his chair in the corner of the last row. He hasn't once looked at the Spanish words written on the board by Ms. Alvarez. When asked why he isn't copying the words in a notebook like the other students, Alphonse avoids eye contact with the teacher, shrugs his shoulders, and slinks down farther in his seat.

Ms. Alvarez worries about Alphonse. He never responds to her questions in class or to her kind remarks between classes. His cumulative folder indicates he has the ability to learn Spanish, but his poor classwork and incomplete homework present a contrary picture. Ms. Alvarez would like to help Alphonse *someday*. Still, with so many rowdy and disorderly students to worry about, she's relieved that at least Alphonse doesn't add to the disturbance.

Students like Alphonse don't cause as much trouble as those who are seeking attention, power, or revenge. They tend to observe school rules and requirements. The problem is that they seldom interact with teachers and peers. They usually remain isolated in the classroom, in the halls, and in the lunchroom.

Don't mistake a student's temporary withdrawal for avoidance-of-failure behavior. Sometimes a student needs to withdraw temporarily, to look within and regroup forces. Withdrawal becomes a problem when the student consistently engages in such behavior over a period of time, in ways that impede academic and social development.

Active Avoidance-of-Failure Behavior

Unlike other types of misbehavior, avoidance-of-failure behavior is rarely active. The problem seldom lies in what the student is doing but rather in what the student is *not* doing.

The only active avoidance-of-failure behavior is the frustration tantrum. On the surface this tantrum resembles a temper tantrum: young students kick and cry, and older students pound the desk and utter unprintable words. The goal of each type of tantrum is different, however. The temper tantrum is an external combustion designed to get the teacher to back off and to submit to the student's demands. In contrast, the frustration tantrum is an implosion designed to let off steam and to focus away from an apparent or potential failure. Students who have frustration tantrums have set out to perform certain tasks but have been unable to succeed to their own satisfaction. Finally, out of sheer frustration, they turn up the vocal volume or collapse into tears, hoping that the emotional outburst will allow them to avoid facing their failure.

Passive Avoidance-of-Failure Behavior

Procrastination

Some students—especially bright, capable youngsters—use procrastination to avoid failure. "I could have if I would have" is their motto. Most people have used this motto on a few occasions. Did you ever delay writing a paper until the night before it was due? If you received a C on that paper, what did you tell yourself? Probably something like this: "I'm really a good student, and I could have gotten an A if I had worked harder." If instead you had worked for weeks on the paper and still received a C, you might have thought, "If this is the best I can do, I must not be as bright as I assumed I was." If you had more such experiences, you might be unwilling to risk an all-out effort again. Why not procrastinate and end up feeling like a winner, instead of working hard and feeling like a failure?

Noncompletion

Neglecting to complete projects and assignments is another variation of avoidance-of-failure behavior. Projects that are never finished cannot be judged or graded, so failure is impossible. I laughed when I learned about this kind of avoidance behavior because at the time I had a drawer full of half-sewn garments. I was not skilled at sewing, but I believed that smart people sewed to avoid the high cost of clothing. I told myself, "I'm really okay at this. Someday I'll finish the clothes." If I had actually finished the sewing and nothing had fit, I'd have had to tell myself, "I guess I'm really a failure at sewing." By not completing the projects, I was able to continue feeling competent.

Temporary Incapacity

Some students avoid failure by developing temporary incapacities. For example, consider the students who are skilled academically but klutzy in physical education classes. When it's time for gym, they may complain of a headache, stomach cramps, nausea—any ailment that might excuse them from a situation in which they do poorly. Since they don't participate in the activity, no one can judge their performance. Of course, their illness disappears as soon as gym class is over.

Assumed Disabilities

The current emphasis on learning disabilities inadvertently helps students successfully carry out avoidance-of-failure behavior. The whole notion of disabilities, especially when drugs are used as part of the corrective procedures, feeds into the students' notion of "I can't" and gives them a seemingly legitimate excuse to withdraw and quit trying.

Even the most astute diagnostician has difficulty differentiating between real disabilities and assumed disabilities. Some students are so good at pretending, even on tests, that teachers often wonder if students can't or if they simply won't. Frequently, the students themselves don't really know. To make matters more confusing, some students who do have a minor disability have learned to make a mountain out of a molehill. By appearing to be more disabled than they are, these students can keep teachers at bay and thus avoid more failure.

Some students are "differently abled" and do need special help to learn. Labels tend to reinforce such children's notions of their inadequacy, however. What they need is to be taught with methods and materials adapted to their needs and to hear the message, "You can do it!" When they receive consistent encouragement, their self-esteem will grow and they'll have less need to work at avoiding failure.

Teacher and Student Response Clues

Teacher Response to Behavior

We can take two readings of our emotional gauge to help us identify whether the goal of a student's misbehavior is avoidance-of-failure. One reading concerns our feelings about the misbehavior. When facing avoidance-of-failure behavior, we feel a mixture of emotions that I call professional concern. We feel sad and helpless because we seem unable to help the student, and we feel defeated because our attempts have failed. Since this behavior rarely disrupts our classroom, we don't experience the kind of negative or unpleasant feelings that accompany the other categories of misbehavior.

The second reading of our emotional gauge concerns our initial action impulse, or how we're tempted to immediately deal with the behavior. When confronted with avoidance-of-failure behavior, our first impulse may be prescriptive—obtaining help from student services personnel—or it may be to resign ourselves to failure since our efforts don't seem to effect change.

Student Response to Intervention

When we intervene with students engaged in avoidance-of-failure behavior, they react in a dependent way. Since they feel incapable of succeeding, they wait for us to give special help rather than taking action themselves. These students do not respond to our requests. No matter what we ask them to do, they continue to do nothing.

Origins of Avoidance-of-Failure Behavior

Rule of the Red Pencil

A long-accepted educational practice has been to mark students' mistakes in red pencil, with the number wrong clearly circled at the top of the page. Students know their mistakes are going to receive attention. Often everyone else in the class knows just how many mistakes they've made. No wonder some students simply decide not to do any work. The rule of the red pencil stems from the belief

At times, students go to such lengths to procrastinate that we may not realize their goal is to avoid failure.

that if children are made to confront mistakes, they will be motivated to avoid repeating the errors. Today, psychologists maintain that just the opposite is true.[1] To motivate children to change their behavior, attention should be turned away from their mistakes and focused instead on their successes.

Unreasonable Expectations

When parents, teachers, or students have unreasonable expectations for success, avoidance-of-failure behavior soon follows. The students, realizing they can't reach the goal, simply refuse to try. They'd rather be chastised for not making the effort than branded "stupid" for trying and failing. They may see peers or siblings succeeding easily, and when they compare their own stumbling efforts, they come up short. Even though we try to tell these students that we'll be satisfied if they put forth their best effort, they're convinced that just trying is not enough. To refuse to try is less damaging to their ego than to try to achieve results that might not be satisfactory.

Perfectionism

Students who strive to be perfect can't tolerate the slightest mistake. They don't see errors as a normal part of the learning process but rather as a tragedy to be avoided at all costs. How sad that so many bright, capable young people refuse to put forth any effort because they believe that only perfect performance is acceptable.

Star Mentality

Society and schools usually recognize only results, rarely the effort involved. For instance, letters are awarded only to athletes who achieve, never to the ones who try hardest. The class valedictorian is honored for earning the highest grades, regardless of whether she or he had to work to get them. In contrast, no one recognizes students like Tony McGuyver, who went from a D-minus to a B-plus average by spending every afternoon with tutors, and Whitney Jackson, who now comes to class on time and pays attention nearly the whole period. Where is their recognition?

Until recognition is accorded to achievements that represent significant steps forward for students, avoidance-of-failure behaviors will continue to be fostered.

Emphasis on Competition

An emphasis on competition in the classroom is another reason some students adopt avoidance-of-failure behavior. If they have to be branded a winner or loser, they'd rather not play at all. Some educators are champions of competition. They believe that competition motivates students to try harder and prepares them for real-life competition. What these educators fail to recognize is that real-life competition differs from classroom competition, particularly in one major aspect: choice of arena. When we compete in the workplace, we are in our chosen career, a career for which we usually have a preference and an aptitude, factors that give a competitive edge. For example, when I propose a book to a publisher, I know I'm competing against other authors, but I also know that I have the talent for writing such a book and hence a reasonable chance for success. I would never tell a clothing manufacturer, "I'd like to design dresses for you." Why should I damage my self-esteem by attempting to do something for which I have no aptitude?

Students, however, are placed in this unfortunate position constantly. All day long, they're compared with other students in different subjects and skills, from math to English to social studies to science to physical education. They don't get to choose which subjects they'd like to compete in and which they'd rather not. They aren't allowed to say "No thank you, Mr. Umbermeyer, but I don't wish to compete in English today." So they speak with their behavior instead. They withdraw, isolate themselves, and refuse to try.

HOW AMAZING...WHAT A SHAME... ANOTHER CASE OF LARYNGITIS, AND JUST BEFORE YOUR ORAL REPORT. WELL, WHAT CAN I SAY?

Some students avoid failure by developing temporary incapacities.

Avoidance-of-Failure Behavior's Silver Lining

For some students, ambition is the silver lining in avoidance-of-failure behavior. They want to succeed in school—if they can be assured of not making mistakes and of achieving some status. With the right strategies, we can nurture this ambition and help the students change their behavior.

For many students with avoidance-of-failure behaviors, however, there is no silver lining. These students are too discouraged. They have incredibly low self-esteem, and they lack the support of friends. Since they have no resources for going it alone, they need and deserve immediate help.

Principles of Prevention

Keeping in mind two principles of prevention is helpful for alleviating avoidance-of-failure behavior. The first principle is to encourage students to change their self-perception from "I can't" to "I can" (Chapter 14). The second principle concerns helping end the students' social isolation by drawing them into congenial relationships with us and with other students (Chapter 15).

Take Step 2: Identify the Goal of the Misbehavior

The goal of the student's misbehavior is entered under Step 2 of the School Action Plan. To determine whether the student employs avoidance-of-failure behavior, use the Chapter 12 Chart as a guide to assessing the behavior descriptions that you've listed under Step 1 of the plan. This chart summarizes the key information about avoidance-of-failure behavior that's presented in this chapter. Another chart that enables you to evaluate the characteristics of avoidance-of-failure behavior in conjunction with those of attention, power, and revenge behaviors is presented in Appendix A, Review Chart of the Four Goals of Misbehavior.

The teacher and student response clues are most helpful in deciding whether avoidance is the goal of misbehavior. Take note of your feelings and your initial action impulse when the student misbehaves, and also how the student responds when you intervene to stop the behavior. The teacher and student response clues to each of the four goals of misbehavior are summarized in Appendix B, Teacher and Student Response Clues to Identifying the Goal of Misbehavior, a handy reference for double-checking identification of a particular goal.

Note

1. Benjamin Bloom, *All Our Children Learning* (New York: McGraw-Hill, 1981), 138.

Characteristics of Avoidance-of-Failure Behavior

Active Avoidance-of-Failure Behavior	*Frustration tantrum:* Student loses control when the pressure to succeed becomes too intense.
Passive Avoidance-of-Failure Behavior	Student procrastinates, fails to complete projects, develops temporary incapacity, or assumes behaviors that resemble a learning disability.
Teacher Response to Behavior	*Feelings:* Professional concern. *Action impulse:* Prescriptive or resigned to failure.
Student Response to Intervention	*Response style:* Dependent. *Response action:* Continues to do nothing.
Origins of Behavior	Rule of the red pencil. Unreasonable expectations of parents and teachers. Student's belief that only perfectionism is acceptable. Star mentality. Emphasis on competition in the classroom.
Silver Lining	Student may want to succeed if he or she can be assured of not making mistakes and of achieving some status. For some severely discouraged students, there is no silver lining.
Principles of Prevention	Encourage student to change self-perception from "I can't" to "I can." Help end student's social isolation by drawing the student into congenial relationships with us and other students.

Investigating Avoidance-of-Failure Behavior

1 Give examples of active and passive avoidance-of-failure behaviors that you've observed in your classroom.

_____

_____

_____

2 Do you agree with the suggested origins of avoidance-of-failure behavior? Why or why not?

_____

_____

_____

3 The silver lining in avoidance-of-failure behavior is that students may have ambition that can be nurtured. Do you agree with this statement? Why or why not?

_____

_____

_____

4 Complete this sentence: When I was a child, one way in which I tried to avoid failure

was _____

_____

_____

_____

CHAPTER 13
When the Goal Is Avoidance-of-Failure: Interventions

We can rarely pinpoint the exact moment of avoidance-of-failure behavior since such behavior usually doesn't disrupt our lessons, distract our attention, or destroy property. Students who fear failure simply don't do their schoolwork, quietly hoping we won't notice.

As discussed in Chapter 12, students who engage in avoidance-of-failure behavior don't believe they can ever belong in a significant way. They don't feel capable, and they probably don't know how to successfully connect or contribute. While we eventually need to help them connect and contribute to make a real difference in their school performance, our first step is to help them feel capable.

Intervention techniques that help students feel capable can be grouped under eight strategies:

- Modify instructional methods.
- Provide tutoring.
- Teach positive self-talk.
- Make mistakes okay.
- Build confidence.
- Focus on past success.
- Make learning tangible.
- Recognize achievement.

The First Three Strategies

Strategies 1 through 3 are specifically tailored to students who fear failure. The other five intervention strategies are also encouragement strategies. They are helpful for all children but particularly useful with students fearful of failure. The five strategies are summarized later in this chapter and fully explained in Chapter 14.

Modify Instructional Methods

Two techniques are recommended for modifying instructional methods: use concrete learning materials and computer-assisted instruction, and teach one step at a time.

Use Concrete Learning Materials and Computer-Assisted Instruction

Many students, particularly young ones, learn best when they use materials that they can see, feel, and manipulate. Over sixty years ago, Maria Montessori proved that children considered failures by their parents and teachers could, with the right materials, learn as well as their so-called brighter peers. To produce these spectacular results, Montessori designed and used concrete learning materials that met these criteria:

Attractive—Children love working with materials that are interesting and colorful.

Self-explanatory—Children are motivated to work when they can determine independently how the materials are used.

Self-correcting—Children discover that making mistakes is natural and okay when no one else has to know how many errors they make while learning a new skill.

Reusable—Children can practice tasks over and over again until they've achieved mastery. Then the same materials can be used again to give children the joy of succeeding repeatedly.

Learning materials that meet Montessori's four criteria are readily available for today's classroom. Moreover, modern technology has provided an additional learning tool that adds a new dimension to teaching methods—the computer. Although not concrete, educational software does have the characteristics of the Montessori learning materials: it is attractive, self-explanatory, self-correcting, and reusable. Students who wouldn't dream of picking up a pencil in class can sit for hours in front of a monitor, working on basic skills.

Computers can't take our place, of course. But as teaching aids for basic skills, computers are hard to beat. Although all students can benefit from computer-assisted instruction, those who underachieve for fear of failure are particularly aided by it. The self-explanatory, self-correcting, and reusable features enable such students to take risks that they'd never chance with traditional instructional materials.

Teach One Step at a Time

Students who are afraid of failure are easily overwhelmed. They can be frightened into passivity by a complex learning task that's appropriate for their classmates. We can entice these students to tackle the task if we break it up into small, progressive steps so that the chance of making errors is reduced. We can further help them by giving feedback after they complete each step. Each small success will spur them on, and each small mistake will be easier to correct than multiple mistakes involving the whole task.

Provide Tutoring

Many students who exhibit fear-of-failure behavior are caught in the failure chain.[1] They have missed learning some basic academic skills, and this gap in skills makes schoolwork difficult and frustrating. Moreover, these students have lost confidence in trying to close the gap because they see classmates completing assignments with ease. As their confidence slips, so does their motivation, which leads to continued poor performance and more erosion of confidence. At this point, the students can do little on their own to break the failure chain. Their best hope is tutoring in basic skills, which breaks the chain by erasing the gap, restoring confidence, and encouraging success. These are some of the forms of tutoring that are most beneficial for students who fear failure:

Extra Help from Teachers

Most teachers can hardly find time to prepare lesson plans and perform clerical duties during "free" periods, lunch, or after school. If we can manage to squeeze out a few extra moments, we can provide individual instruction. If, however, we are simply smothered under an avalanche of extras, we need to acknowledge this reality and seek help elsewhere for students who need it.

Remediation Programs

Although many students with fear-of-failure behavior have normal-range IQs and no apparent disability, some are genuinely disabled. Diagnostic testing is called for when we suspect that a student might qualify for an in-school remediation program.

Adult Volunteers

Many school districts maintain a corps of adult volunteers who come to the school two or three times a week to work with students. Volunteers who are trained in both instructional and encouragement techniques, who are reliable, and who can be supervised by teachers, administrators, or counselors may be able to provide tutoring for students whose academic deficits are not too great.

Peer Tutoring

Many districts have established programs in which students can help other students with academics. Both tutor and tutee can benefit greatly from such programs.

Learning Centers

Adult volunteer and peer tutoring usually take place during regular school hours, which means that students may miss classroom instruction. That's one reason for the recent growth of commercial learning centers that offer individualized learning experiences after school, on weekends, or during vacation periods. Such centers are staffed by personnel who have the time and the training to provide in-depth diagnostic testing so that tutoring can be tailored to a student's needs. The best centers provide a variety of both concrete and abstract learning materials and guarantee a low teacher-student ratio, which allows one-step-at-a-time teaching that reinforces each success a student achieves. Many young people find that learning comes much more easily outside of the competitive school setting, in a new place where they have not repeatedly experienced failure.

Everyone can benefit from positive self-talk.

Teach Positive Self-Talk

Students with avoidance-of-failure behavior often develop a pattern of negative self-talk. When faced with tasks, they may repeatedly think, "I can't do this" or "It's too hard" or "I'll never get this right." Such damaging put-downs can become self-fulfilling prophecies that stifle students' initiative and motivation to learn. We can help students turn negative internal messages into positive self-talk by using several techniques.

Post Positive Classroom Signs

"You can if you think you can!" was the message on the sign posted by Mrs. Jones, my ninth-grade algebra teacher way back when. I read that sign every day, and its positive words gradually affected my subconscious persuasion that I'd never do well in algebra. Little by little, the impact of my own negative self-talk was reduced, and my willingness to persevere with mathematics increased.

Plastering our classroom walls with positive self-talk signs takes little effort. Students can be asked to write—and perhaps illustrate—a number of such signs that can be rotated on a regular basis. Here are some possible messages for the signs:

- I can do it!
- With a little effort, I'll succeed.
- I'm smart enough to do good work.
- I can when I tell myself I can.
- I can change how I think and feel.

Require Two "Put-Ups" for Every Put-Down

Initiate the rule that for every negative statement students say aloud about themselves, they must counter with two "put-ups," or positive statements. Such a practice not only helps students focus on the way they talk about themselves but also helps transform a negative self-image into a positive one. At first, students may feel a little foolish about verbalizing good things about themselves. But with time and practice, put-ups usually become just as automatic as put-downs, and when this happens, the fear of failure diminishes.

Encourage Positive Self-Talk Before Beginning Tasks

The tape recorder in students' heads begins playing as soon as an assignment is given. To ensure that the tape played is positive, we can ask students with avoidance-of-failure behavior to say aloud two positive things about the task at hand, such as "I can do these problems with fractions" and "I'm smart enough to find all the answers."

If students get bogged down during the assignment, we can suggest that they repeat their positive statements under their breath. Students who learn to consciously "replay" the positive tape when they feel threatened by a task will usually achieve success. That success will make it easier to "eject" the negative tape and to insert the positive tape whenever they're dealing with an assignment.

Five Additional Intervention Strategies: An Overview

Five intervention strategies that are also encouragement strategies useful with all students are especially helpful in working with those who fear failure. Explanations of the specific techniques relating to each of these strategies are presented in Chapter 14.

Make Mistakes Okay

The fear of making mistakes keeps students stuck in the avoidance-of-failure rut. They interpret every mistake they make, no matter how large or small, as proof that they can't do anything right—ever. We can help them learn to accept mistakes as part of the learning process. Techniques for helping students accept mistakes are:

- Talk about mistakes.
- Equate mistakes with effort.
- Minimize the effect of making mistakes.

Build Confidence

Building confidence means helping students who fear failure realize that success is possible. They need to believe they not only can perform tasks capably but also are successful just being themselves, regardless of their skill level. Use these techniques to help build confidence:

- Focus on improvement.
- Notice contributions.

- Build on strengths.
- Show faith in students.
- Acknowledge the difficulty of a task.
- Set time limits on tasks.

Focus on Past Success

Every student has experienced some success, although we may have to dig deeply to find examples for students who avoid failure. Their scholastic output is often minimal because of their passivity. But by repeatedly reminding these students of past successes, no matter how small, we can build a basis for effort that may lead to major achievements. Try these techniques to help focus on students' past success:

- Analyze past success.
- Repeat past success.

Make Learning Tangible

If they can't see or touch something, many students think it doesn't exist. Unfortunately, "learning" is something that's hard to see or touch. For students who need sensory feedback to realize that learning has occurred, we have to make learning as tangible as possible. To make learning tangible, use the following ideas:

- "I-Can" cans.
- Accomplishment Albums.
- Checklists of skills.
- Flowchart of concepts.
- Talks about yesterday, today, and tomorrow.

Recognize Achievement

If students were to receive as much recognition for achievement as they do for failure, avoidance-of-failure behavior could be eliminated. Achievement or improvement in any area—no matter how seemingly insignificant—needs to be acknowledged. When students fearful of failure receive recognition from others, especially from teachers and classmates, they begin to feel capable and to believe that they can successfully connect and contribute. Techniques to help recognize students' achievements are:

- Applause.
- Clapping and standing ovations.
- Stars and stickers.
- Awards and assemblies.
- Exhibits.
- Positive time-out.
- Self-approval.

Take Step 3: Choose Intervention Techniques

If you've determined that the student who's the subject of your School Action Plan has avoidance-of-failure as his or her goal, select several of the intervention techniques described in this chapter and listed in the Chapter 13 Chart. For a full explanation of the intervention techniques that are also encouragement strategies, read Chapter 14.

Make your intervention choices on the basis of these factors:

- the student's age
- what makes the most sense to you
- what fits your teaching style and personality

Record the selected techniques under Step 3 of the School Action Plan.

As you complete this step, keep in mind that intervention does not mean punishment. Instead, think of intervention as guidance with a double purpose: to stop the behavior occurring at the moment and to influence the student to choose more appropriate behavior in the future.

A summary chart that includes interventions recommended for each of the four goals of misbehavior is presented in Appendix C, Summary Chart of Interventions.

Note

1. The failure chain concept was developed by Dr. Ray Huntington, president of Huntington Learning Centers, Inc.

Interventions for Avoidance-of-Failure Behavior

General Strategy	Techniques
Modify instructional methods.	Use concrete learning materials and computer-assisted instruction. Teach one step at a time.
Provide tutoring.	Extra help from teachers. Remediation programs. Adult volunteers. Peer tutoring. Learning centers.
Teach positive self-talk.	Post positive classroom signs. Require two "put-ups" for every put-down. Encourage positive self-talk before beginning tasks.
Make mistakes okay.	Talk about mistakes. Equate mistakes with effort. Minimize the effect of making mistakes.
Build confidence.	Focus on improvement. Notice contributions. Build on strengths. Show faith in students. Acknowledge the difficulty of a task. Set time limits on tasks.
Focus on past success.	Analyze past success. Repeat past success.
Make learning tangible.	"I-Can" cans. Accomplishment Albums. Checklists of skills. Flowchart of concepts. Talks about yesterday, today, and tomorrow.
Recognize achievement.	Applause. Clapping and standing ovations. Stars and stickers. Awards and assemblies. Exhibits. Positive time-out. Self-approval.

6

SECTION SIX

Taking Supportive Action: Building Self-Esteem

We can help students feel connected with us by forming A+ relationships with them. An A+ relationship is one that involves plenty of *acceptance, attention, appreciation, affirmation,* and *affection*. When we model these five A's, we teach students how to initiate and maintain positive relationships with their peers, and we encourage them to become receptive to our efforts to discipline, to instruct, or to help in other ways.

CHAPTER 14
Helping Students Feel Capable

If our discipline program were to include only intervention strategies for the moment of misbehavior, we could be pretty sure that students would misbehave again—today, tomorrow, or the next day. The only way to end the misbehavior permanently is to raise students' self-esteem. The building blocks of self-esteem are the same three Cs that help students feel they belong (Chapter 2). When students believe they're *capable* and know they can *connect* and *contribute* successfully, they no longer need to engage in misbehavior to try to fulfill their need to belong.

We can teach students to satisfy the three Cs through using encouragement strategies. Our positive response to appropriate behavior can do more to convince students to continue such behavior than will all the interventions in the world. Fortunately, most encouragement strategies are neither difficult nor time-consuming. We simply need to be aware of them and committed to using them daily.

As we implement encouragement strategies, we need to recognize that an important variable affects our ability to give encouragement—our emotional response toward a particular misbehavior. For example, giving over and above the normal level of encouragement to students fearing failure is usually easy even though it's time-consuming. Such students don't disrupt our classroom, so our response to them is concerned and sympathetic. We naturally want to help them. On the other hand, giving encouragement at even the normal level to power-seeking students may seem to be an insurmountable amount to us. This is because our emotional response to these students is negative. Their behavior disrupts our classroom and causes us to feel anger and frustration.

If we keep in mind that our emotional response varies according to the behavior in action, we will feel less discouraged as we try to encourage our students, particularly those seeking power or revenge.

Motivator of Success: The "I-Can" Level

One of the most accurate predictors of success in school is a student's "I-can" level. The I-can level is a much more helpful motivator than the IQ level. Students who believe in their ability to master required learning tasks usually succeed (assuming the teaching methods and materials are appropriate to their stage of development). Their success is not only academic but also emotional. They feel good about themselves because they've fulfilled one of the three Cs—feeling capable.

We can work toward raising students' I-can levels by using the encouragement techniques described in this chapter. The techniques are grouped according to five major strategies.

Strategy 1: Make Mistakes Okay

The fear of making mistakes undermines a student's I-can level. When we remove this fear, we remove a great barrier to feeling capable. Several effective techniques can help us do this.

Talk about mistakes. Young people are often selective in their observations. They notice their own mistakes but not those of others. As a result, they become convinced that everyone else is better, smarter, and more capable than they. Our job is to revise this viewpoint by helping students understand that everyone makes mistakes, that nobody is perfect.

When students begin to talk about mistakes, they soon discover that making mistakes is a natural part of the learning process. The game of "Classroom Password" provides an easy format for initiating such discussion. When the bell rings to signal lunch or to change classes, we can stand at the door and announce that the password for leaving is to state one recent mistake. Any mistake will do, whether it occurred at home, on the school bus, or in class.

At first, students probably won't appreciate this game. Since failure is talked about openly so rarely, some students think that if they reveal their mistakes in front of others, a bolt of lightning will zap them on the spot. To understand that

Rewarding mistakes is one way to make the point that effort is valuable even when we fail.

their fear is groundless, students need to hear us admitting that we make mistakes too. By sharing our own mistakes with students, we can help them learn that mistakes are a normal part of everyone's life, and, consequently, they no longer will feel isolated in their ability to mess things up.

When both we and our students become used to talking about mistakes, we can narrow the focus of the password: "Name one mistake you made in (English, algebra, social studies) and what you learned from that mistake." (Of course, we aren't exempt from this password either!) Responding to this password helps students realize that mistakes are an integral part of the learning process.

Eventually, we can expand the password game by adding this question: "What can you do so that you don't make the same mistake again?" Answering this helps students understand that the most important thing is not avoiding mistakes but being able to figure out what to do next. As they hear how others plan to correct mistakes, they discover strategies for dealing with their own mistakes.

Equate mistakes with effort. We need to acknowledge that more mistakes are made by active people than by passive people and that active participation is desirable. Then we can actually reward mistakes with enthusiastic remarks, thus motivating students to continue working. Comments like these are appropriate when students who are really trying make mistakes:

- You've made a mistake. So what? Now, let's see what can be learned from it.
- This mistake is no big deal. After all, if you never made a mistake in (English, algebra, social studies), I wouldn't have a job!

Some astute industry leaders award prizes for creative ideas that fail. Such prizes encourage the divergent thinking and experimentation that often lead to successful innovation. Perhaps such a practice might work in the classroom too.

Minimize the effect of making mistakes. As part of the job, teachers are generally mistake-oriented, assuming the task of correcting students' schoolwork as well as their behavior. Recall the "rule of the red pencil," the long-accepted educational practice of marking mistakes on students' papers in bold red pencil (Chapter 12). To minimize the effect of making mistakes and thus help students feel capable, we need to stop highlighting every error. Red-lined papers can be overwhelming to students, especially those who already have low self-esteem and feel incapable.

This doesn't mean that we can't give constructive criticism and ask students to correct mistakes. It just means that we reevaluate the task of correction by breaking it down into easy steps that students are capable of completing. We can do this by having students focus on correcting only one or two errors or types of errors at a time.

Strategy 2: Build Confidence

Students must have the confidence that success is possible. To help them build such confidence, we can use a number of techniques that emphasize positive feedback.

Focus on improvement. If we wait until a student completes a task error-free before we say anything positive, we're likely to wait forever. If instead we devote more interest to the *process* of learning rather than the *product,* we'll notice and praise each small step forward.

The axiom "Anything worth doing is worth doing well" limits potential. After all, I'd never have kissed anyone if I'd had to do it well the first time! A more appropriate slogan to live with, one that encourages the feeling of being capable, is "Anything worth doing is worth doing."

When we note a student's improvement, we focus only on what the student can do today, not on what we hope the student can do tomorrow. We don't compare the student's work with anyone else's or with grade-level charts.

Notice contributions. Students who fear failure may refuse to put down anything on paper, because any errors will be permanently recorded for all to see. Their fear may not extend beyond the edge of the paper, however. Such students often are willing to actively participate in class discussions and group tasks. We can point out the usefulness of these contributions to the students, to their classmates, and to their parents. Since being able to contribute is one of the three Cs of belonging, we need to notice and encourage this behavior as much as possible. One C leads to another—today's contributions boost tomorrow's feelings of capability.

Build on strengths. Every student has some strengths, no matter how well hidden. We talked earlier about seeking the good in each student to be able to build healthy relationships (Chapter 11). Likewise, we can seek out strengths on which to build academic skills. When we notice the gold shining through, we can tell the students directly or write it down on their papers. They need to hear about their strengths frequently and in detail.

While growing up, many of us were told that we'd get "swelled heads" if we bragged or said complimentary things about ourselves. What nonsense! If we can't talk about what we can do well, how can we possibly feel capable? The ability to recognize and talk about our strengths is a powerful motivator and self-esteem builder. We can help students focus on their strengths by playing a variation of Classroom Password, asking each student to mention a personal strength, positive characteristic, or talent before exiting the classroom at the end of the period or the day.

Show faith in students. Our faith in our students is reflected in our expectations. Low expectations demonstrate low confidence. Higher expectations indicate more confidence, as long as the expectations are realistic and the lessons appropriate. To sincerely demonstrate faith in our students' capabilities, we can tailor activities to their abilities. Moreover, positive comments such as "You can handle it," "You are the kind of students who can do this," and "I know you can do it" indicate our faith in our students.

Acknowledge the difficulty of a task. Many students, especially those trying to avoid failure, perceive any new learning task as difficult. We need to acknowledge their point of view. One way to do this is to avoid making light of a task by labeling it "easy." If students do fail at such an "easy" task, they naturally assume that they must be stupid. Instead, we need to support students' feelings while affirming their capabilities: "I know this is difficult. Keep at it a while longer. I bet you'll get the hang of it." When students do succeed at a task that we've labeled "difficult," their self-esteem gets a healthy boost.

Set time limits on tasks. Setting a time limit on tasks that students perceive as difficult can be a helpful technique. When students know that the hard work is not going to last forever, the task can seem easier to bear. Students should recognize that the time limit only refers to how long they must keep working before quitting. If they want to continue working after the time is up, they can be encouraged to do so. Otherwise, the pressure of the time limit will only create more stress and greater resistance.

Strategy 3: Focus on Past Success

When I was growing up, my parents and teachers frequently pointed out what I was doing wrong, with the hope of motivating me to do better in the future. Today, many educational psychologists tell us that just the opposite is true. The way to motivate young people to succeed is to point out everything they do right. Success builds success, we are told, and we therefore should focus on students' past accomplishments to ensure that their good work continues.

Analyze past success. We need to do more than just point out successes, says Bernard Weiner, developer of the attribute theory of success.[1] Weiner states that most of us attribute our successes to five factors:

- our belief in our ability
- our effort
- help from others
- task difficulty
- luck

Students control only two of these factors—their belief in their ability and the amount of effort they put out. They cannot dictate how much help they will receive from others, how difficult the task will be, or whether luck will be on their side.

We can help students understand that the two factors they do control are the major components of success. We can ask them, "Do you know why you succeeded at that task?" If they reply that it was because they have "smarts" or tried so hard, we can reinforce their perceptions by agreeing with them. If their response is because they got help, we can counter, "Yes, that's true, you did get help, but you put out the effort and proved you have the ability." If they say that the task was easy, we can respond, "Your ability and effort made it seem easy." If they claim it was just luck, we can say, "You made your own luck by using your ability and making the effort."

We can also challenge students to repeat the task again so they can prove to themselves that they created their own success. By continually analyzing past successes in this way, we not only help students believe in their own capabilities but also encourage them to keep making the effort to learn.

Repeat past success. While moving forward to new learning tasks is important, standing still for a moment, savoring and repeating today's successes, is equally important. A familiar classroom phenomenon lends credibility to this observation—the enthusiasm that students display for doing old worksheets over and over again.

Many teachers place extra copies of worksheets in a box at the back of the room for students to do again when they have time. Some students will happily complete ten copies of the same old math sheet, but complain bitterly about today's work. When students repeat yesterday's work, they use skills they have mastered, therefore making fewer mistakes and experiencing more success.

Adults also like to repeat past successes. How many of us have a favorite menu for dinner parties that we repeatedly prepare? If we had to try different menus every time we entertained, we'd probably stop inviting guests for dinner to avoid the embarrassment of fallen soufflés and burnt roasts!

Strategy 4: Make Learning Tangible

One reason why some students don't believe in their capabilities is because they can't see their progress. Grades and test scores, the usual benchmarks for measuring progress, don't always give the necessary information. For example, a student who receives Cs for two consecutive marking periods might assume that no progress has been made. Young elementary students often receive only satisfactory or unsatisfactory marks, which reveal nothing about their progress. We need to switch from "Wadja get?" to "Wadja learn?"

"I-Can" cans. Young students can make an I-Can can by decorating a large, empty juice can with contact paper. In their can, they deposit strips of paper on which they've written skills they've mastered, such as reading or spelling words and arithmetic facts. As their can fills up, students can point with pride to all the new things they've learned. The I-Can can also is useful during parent conferences because it contains concrete evidence that a child is making progress.

Young students love the recognition represented by stars and stickers.

Accomplishment Albums. Older students can create an Accomplishment Album[2] using a three-ring binder, paper, theme dividers, and decorations such as stickers and glitter. In their album, within sections marked by dividers with headings such as "Math Problems I Can Solve," "Books I Have Read," "French Verbs I Can Conjugate," students can chart their progress by writing down new skills mastered. The album concept also works well for just one subject area, with the headings reflecting appropriate categories for the subject. For example, an eighth-grade student's English album might include "New Vocabulary I've Mastered," "Grammar and Punctuation Rules I've Learned," "Literature I've Read," and "Writing Skills I've Demonstrated."

Students should never compare their Accomplishment Albums. The emphasis should be solely on individual growth, helping students see what they learned today that they didn't know yesterday. Accomplishment Albums also are great aids during parent conferences since they are tangible records of student progress.

Checklists of skills. Many schools and school systems have established master lists of skills to be taught in each subject at each grade level. Teachers generally use these lists when preparing lessons and when writing reports on student progress for parents. Such checklists also are ideal for helping students feel capable, for with each new skill they can check off, their I-can level rises.

Flowchart of concepts. A flowchart accompanies just about every commercially published academic program. The chart lists concepts and skills introduced in the program and describes where and when they appear. Most teachers primarily use the flowchart to plan lessons, but it can also be used in helping students plot progress. A chart may need to be simplified for use by young students, but even they can benefit from knowing where they are going, when they will get there, and which milestones they will pass along the way.

Talks about yesterday, today, and tomorrow. Useful in conjunction with any of the previous techniques suggested for this strategy are frequent talks about yesterday, today, and tomorrow. For example, we can say to a student, "Remember when you weren't able to spell many words? Now look at how many words you have inside your I-Can can!" When we discuss the progress a student has made in such concrete terms, we increase confidence and self-esteem immeasurably. Moreover, failure doesn't seem so scary or so inevitable when we talk frequently about progress.

Talks about tomorrow based on past successes help students anticipate future success: "Look how many items on the checklist you've mastered this month. How many more do you think you'll be able to master next month?" Such anticipation is an excellent motivator for convincing students to stick to difficult tasks.

Strategy 5: Recognize Achievement

For students to continue to want to make progress, they must receive recognition from others for the progress they've already made. Here are some effective techniques for acknowledging achievements:

Applause. Applause says, "Hooray for you! You did it!" When we give applause, we don't have to clap our hands, but our enthusiasm ought to be no less evident.

We can applaud achievement in school and out, in both academic and nonacademic areas. Applause needs to be specific and nonjudgmental, without comparisons, and with no mention of past or future expectations.

One of the best ways to give applause is to simply notice the situation and reflect it back to the student. "Wow, Monica, look at how clearly you've outlined the causes leading up to the Civil War." "Congratulations, Monroe! I see your sketch was selected as picture of the week in art class."

Applause is called for whenever students exhibit positive behavior in a situation that previously caused them difficulty. For example, we notice that Quentin, who has been withdrawn in gym class, is finally taking an active part in a game. We can reinforce the good example he is setting for himself by saying, "Way to go, Quentin! I saw you cheering on your teammates while waiting for your turn."

Clapping and standing ovations. We can encourage students to recognize classmates' achievements by clapping and giving standing ovations. The recipient feels noticed, appreciated, and special. Most students love taking center stage, even for just a moment. It costs nothing, takes little time, provides a change of pace, and releases pent-up energy for the entire class.

Stars and stickers. Young students love the recognition represented by stars and stickers. A happy face on a worksheet or a big golden star stuck on a shirt collar says, "I've noticed your achievement, and I'm proud of you."

Awards and assemblies. All kinds of certificates and awards can be given out in the homeroom, in the lunchroom, or during assemblies. The more achievements we find to notice, the more positive the classroom atmosphere and the school environment become. Remember, however, to recognize increased effort and improved performance, not just "the best." One clever school staff takes unclaimed sneakers from the lost and found, paints them gold, and presents them to deserving students as "The Golden Sneaker Award for Runaway Effort."

Exhibits. By means of bulletin boards, display cases, and presentations in other classrooms, we can advertise students' achievements. We can also invite parents to view special exhibits of student work, and we can submit announcements of student achievements to the local newspaper.

Positive time-out. Everyone knows that students sent to time-out in the principal's office are in trouble. This negative image of the school administrator can be changed if we start sending students to the office for positive time-out, or to receive recognition for achievement from the principal. We can also send students to counselors, librarians, learning specialists, or volunteers for recognition. Positive time-out is a particularly powerful technique to use with students who are afraid to fail. When these students receive recognition from staff members, their low opinion of themselves starts changing for the better.

Classroom teachers can provide another kind of positive time-out. Taking a moment at the end of class to talk alone with a student who deserves recognition is a powerful motivator. We could also take a few minutes during lunch, free periods, or after school to deliver such praise. We don't have to do anything fancy during positive time-out, and it needn't take long. It's our presence and our undivided attention that mean so much to a student. Even older students appreciate a teacher's attention, although many wouldn't admit it for fear of being labeled "teacher's pet."

Self-approval. Teaching students to recognize their own achievements is vital. Otherwise, students may become approval-dependent, waiting for others to notice what they've done instead of looking inside for self-approval. One way we can promote self-approval is by asking each student to state a personal accomplishment that's worthy of recognition. At first, fulfilling this request may be difficult and embarrassing for many students, especially those who fear failure. In time, however, students not only become accustomed to the procedure but also learn to enjoy the good feelings that spring from talking about their accomplishments.

Begin Step 4: Select Encouragement Techniques to Build Capability

There's no limit to the number of encouragement techniques you can use to help boost the self-esteem of the student who's the subject of your School Action Plan. Begin now by choosing several of the techniques that specifically aid in building feelings of capability. These techniques, which are summarized in the Chapter 14 Chart, are helpful with all students, but they are particularly beneficial for students with avoidance-of-failure behaviors. Because these students have been refusing to try, they need special assistance in raising their I-can level so they'll begin to believe they are capable not only of trying but also of succeeding.

Unlike the interventions, the techniques you select are not tied directly to the goal of the student's misbehavior. Recall some of the student's positive behaviors, and choose techniques that will reinforce those behaviors. After all, you don't want to undo what's going wrong at the expense of ignoring what's going right!

Under Step 4 of the Action Plan, be as specific as possible about each "capable technique" you've chosen. Note how and when you think you'll use the technique. The more details you include, the more effective your plan will be.

Remember that under Step 4, you'll also be adding ways in which you can help the student *connect* (Chapter 15) as well as encouragement techniques that help the student *contribute* successfully (Chapter 16).

A summary chart of all the encouragement techniques is presented in Appendix D, The Building Blocks of Self-Esteem.

Notes

1. Bernard Weiner, "Principles for a Theory of Student Motivation and Their Application Within an Attributional Framework," in *Research on Motivation in Education: Student Motivation,* Volume I, eds. R. E. Ames and C. Ames (New York: Academic Press, 1984).

2. Linda Albert and Michael Popkin, *Quality Parenting* (New York: Random House, 1987), 105-106.

CHAPTER 14 CHART
Helping Students Feel Capable

General Strategy	*Techniques*
Make mistakes okay.	Talk about mistakes. Equate mistakes with effort. Minimize the effect of making mistakes.
Build confidence.	Focus on improvement. Notice contributions. Build on strengths. Show faith in students. Acknowledge the difficulty of a task. Set time limits on tasks.
Focus on past success.	Analyze past success. Repeat past success.
Make learning tangible.	"I-Can" cans. Accomplishment Albums. Checklists of skills. Flowchart of concepts. Talks about yesterday, today, and tomorrow.
Recognize achievement.	Applause. Clapping and standing ovations. Stars and stickers. Awards and assemblies. Exhibits. Positive time-out. Self-approval.

Helping Students Feel Capable

Below are the techniques suggested for helping students feel capable. Next to each, write the symbols that are correct for you:

> * Indicates technique you are currently using
> **A** Indicates technique that is appropriate for your students
> **?** Indicates technique you need clarified or want to think about for a while
> **T** Indicates technique for which you'd like more training
> **X** Indicates new technique that you plan to use in the next month

Strategy 1: Make mistakes okay.

_____ Talk about mistakes.

_____ Equate mistakes with effort.

_____ Minimize the effect of making mistakes.

Strategy 2: Build confidence.

_____ Focus on improvement.

_____ Notice contributions.

_____ Build on strengths.

_____ Show faith in students.

_____ Acknowledge the difficulty of a task.

_____ Set time limits on tasks.

Strategy 3: Focus on past success.

_____ Analyze past success.

_____ Repeat past success.

Strategy 4: Make learning tangible.

_____ "I-Can" cans.

_____ Accomplishment Albums.

_____ Checklists of skills.

_____ Flowchart of concepts.

_____ Talks about yesterday, today, and tomorrow.

Strategy 5: Recognize achievement.

_____ Applause.

_____ Clapping and standing ovations.

_____ Stars and stickers.

_____ Awards and assemblies.

_____ Exhibits.

_____ Positive time-out.

_____ Self-approval.

Helping Students Connect

We can help students feel connected with us by forming A+ relationships with them. An A+ relationship is one that involves plenty of *acceptance, attention, appreciation, affirmation,* and *affection*. When we model these five A's, we teach students how to initiate and maintain positive relationships with their peers, and we encourage them to become receptive to our efforts to discipline, to instruct, or to help in other ways. When we withhold the A's, students are likely to become hostile and uncooperative. This chapter discusses how we can administer doses of the A's in various ways that help students connect.

The Five A's

Acceptance

"The most critical behavior a child can experience is total acceptance as a person. . . . it is . . . the most growth-producing gift that can be given," writes Barbara Clark in *Growing Up Gifted*.[1] Even though we know that growth is an essential function of learning, we can't base our acceptance of students on the growth that they might make or should make or must make. We need to accept them wholeheartedly as they are right now—complete with quirks, flaws, and faults. Acceptance of each student must be sincere and unconditional.

Acceptance is like an umbrella over the other four A's. It is the essential attitude that allows us to freely give attention, appreciation, affirmation, and affection. When we demonstrate these other A's, we can be sure that students feel accepted.

Accepting the Doer, Not the Deed
Chapter 9 includes advice about how we can voice disapproval of a deed without rejecting the doer. Students need to believe they are still worthy human beings even when their behavior is inappropriate. This helps them retain enough self-esteem so they're able to choose more appropriate behavior in the future.

Accepting Students' Personal Style
When students started showing up in my class wearing safety pins in their ears and sporting pink hairdos, I admit I was a little taken aback. These students offended my personal taste, although I suppose my polyester pantsuits may have offended their sense of aesthetics in turn. Personal idiosyncrasies in dress or

habits require a tolerant attitude. If individual quirks get in the way of classroom functioning, however, we may have to work out some kind of compromise with the students. But we need to remember that values do change from generation to generation and what seems unacceptable to us may be the only way that students can fit in with their peers.

Attention

We give attention by making ourselves available to students, by sharing our time and our energy in meaningful ways. We can prevent a lot of classroom disruption by providing large doses of positive attention before misbehavior occurs. The time we take away from teaching to give attention is balanced by the time we save when we don't have to cope with misbehavior.

How can one teacher give personal attention to a class of twenty to thirty-five students and still cover the curriculum? Fortunately, it's not the quantity of our attention that counts but the quality. Some of the ways in which we can give quality attention require only a few moments, and yet the beneficial effects can be felt for hours or even days.

Greet Students

The quickest and easiest way to make sure each student has a small bit of quality attention from us is to use the few moments before or after class to say a word or two to each individually. Yes, this means we must be organized enough so that we don't need these few moments for last-minute preparation or cleanup, but the extra effort is worth it. We're sure to get results, as Ms. Aylers discovered when she gave some quality attention to one of her kindergartners:

Elliot was the class bully. Nothing Ms. Aylers did or said seemed to reach him. I suggested that she try giving him special attention by greeting him each morning with a compliment. Ms. Aylers seemed doubtful that she could find anything nice to say to Elliot, so I suggested that she comment on his shirt—the color, the design, the buttons, whatever caught her eye. A few days later, she sent me a one-word message: HELP! I asked her what was wrong. "It's about Elliot," she replied. "He was so proud that I noticed his shirt, he hasn't changed it all week! He's beginning to smell, and the other kids hold their noses when he comes into the room. Now what do I do?"

Greetings can be just as effective with older students, although they may not let us know how much they appreciate our attention.

At my suggestion, Mr. Lambeth started using farewells with his eighth graders. After a week with no student feedback, he complained that the technique wasn't working. I suggested that he stop for a few days and see what happened. Sure enough, the day he ceased saying good-bye, Kimberly Ann, a student in his first-period class, stopped by to ask him why he was mad at everyone. When he assured her he wasn't angry, she replied, "Then why didn't you stand at the door and say good-bye to us like you usually do?"

Listen to Students

I suspect that the most powerful way to give attention is to listen when students have something on their minds they want to talk about. The topic may range from classroom concerns to problems with peers to family troubles. Listening to students requires more time than quick greetings, but even one fifteen-minute session can cement the teacher-student connection for the entire year.

Many teachers have difficulty listening to students talk about their problems. This discomfort stems from an incorrect belief that we must solve all the problems that students bring to us. The role of the teacher who listens is simply to provide a sympathetic ear. When we use good listening skills, we can help students talk through their concerns, and we can encourage them to create solutions. Good listening is a skill that everyone can develop. Here are some of the basics:

Keep quiet. When we don't know what to say, saying nothing is probably best. When we do know what to say, we need to be careful not to say it prematurely. We should interrupt only when necessary, such as when we need to slow down the student so we can understand what's being said.

Give nonverbal signals to show interest. Make eye contact. Lean toward the student. Give an occasional nod. Assuming a physical posture similar to the student's sometimes helps the student feel comfortable with us.

Verbalize interest without words. Use encouraging sounds such as "Uh-huh" or "Mmmm," while keeping tone of voice and body language friendly.

Reflect back what the student has said. By paraphrasing in our own words what we think we've heard, we tell the student we're on the same wavelength. If we've misinterpreted, the student will correct us.

Ask questions sparingly. Use questions only to draw out more information, to clarify what's been said, or to help the student see possible solutions to the problem.

Seek out the student's feelings. The emotional content of the student's message is the real communication. We can ask for his or her feelings directly: "How do you feel about _____?" Or we can make a tentative guess about the feelings, and let the student correct us if we're wrong. We need to remind the student that all feelings are okay, even negative emotions. Sometimes we need to help the student distinguish between feelings, which are all acceptable, and actions, which are not all acceptable.

Teach Students to Ask for Attention

Wouldn't it be wonderful if students were willing to ask us for attention rather than misbehaving to get our attention? Even though we're not always able to provide attention at the precise moment students feel the need, we can promise that our attention will be available in the near future. We can keep a datebook or sign-up sheet for students who want to request an "attention date." Once students know when we'll be able to give them special attention, they usually are satisfied to wait.

A Potpourri of Ideas for Giving Attention

During inservice workshops, I've asked teachers how they pay special attention to students. Here are some of their ideas:

- Spend time chatting with students in the hall after class.
- Ask students about their life outside school.
- Remember what students talk to you about, and mention these things when appropriate.

Giving attention when it's not expected can help keep a student on track.

- Eat in the cafeteria with the students occasionally.
- Invite students, a few at a time, to eat lunch with you in your room.
- Attend school athletic, musical, and theatrical events.
- Get involved in a community project with your students.
- Schedule individual conferences with students.
- Join the students on the playground occasionally.
- Chaperon school events once in a while.
- Recognize birthdays in some way.
- Make bulletin boards with the students' baby pictures.
- Send cards, messages, homework to absent students.
- Express real interest in students' work or hobbies

Appreciation

According to psychologist William James, "The deepest principle of human nature is the craving to be appreciated." To show students that we appreciate them, we can state how something they've done has benefited us, the class, or the school. Appreciation differs from applause (Chapter 14) in that the focus is on the contribution made rather than just on the act or accomplishment. Our appreciation needs to be spoken loudly and displayed clearly, for as Mark Twain put it: "The compliment that helps us on our way is not the one that is shut up in the mind, but the one that is spoken out."

Appreciation is often mistakenly confused with encouragement. As we're finding out, encouragement is a process involving many esteem-building techniques, of which appreciation is only one.

Appreciate the Deed, Not the Doer

Appreciation in itself isn't harmful, but its misuse may have harmful effects. For example, many of us have praised our students to the heavens and then watched their behavior deteriorate in minutes. The deterioration does not stem from the appreciation itself but from the manner in which it has been given. Appreciation is bestowed incorrectly when it addresses the doer in subjective terms. Judgmental words and evaluative statements become the catalyst that causes misbehavior to follow words of praise.

When we use appreciation correctly, we address the deed, not the doer. By focusing on the deed, we attach praise to the behavior that we wish to see continued. The student then knows exactly what she or he has done to gain our appreciation, which increases the chance that the student will repeat the same or similar behavior. Here are the techniques necessary for effective use of appreciation:

Describe the behavior accurately. To show appreciation of a student's deeds, we need to accurately pinpoint and describe behavior. The same test for objectivity that we use to describe misbehavior can be applied to good behavior: Can our description of good behavior be documented by a video camera? Statements such as "Keep up the good work" or "Thanks for helping out" do not pass the documentary test. These general platitudes do not tell students exactly what they have done to earn the praise and, consequently, are ineffective in helping students continue to choose good behavior.

Use three-part appreciation statements. Once we have pinpointed the behavior, we can state our appreciation for it in the form of a three-part statement that describes:

1. the student's action
2. how we feel about the action
3. the positive effect of the action

- Anthony, when you clean up the science lab, I feel delighted, because it saves me time.
- Marylissa, when you complete your reading assignments on time like you did today, I feel great, because then the whole class can stay on schedule.

When we give appreciation statements, we help students recognize the specific beneficial effects of their actions, which encourages them to keep behaving positively.

Focus only on the present. Appreciation statements are best received when they focus on the present moment. Saying "Anthony, how come you never cleaned the science lab before?" will only make Anthony feel discouraged about his past failings instead of proud of his present achievement. Similarly, any statement of future expectations can scare away the student. If we say, "Anthony, now I expect that every Friday afternoon you'll clean the science lab as well as you did today," Anthony is likely to be sorry he ever swabbed a test tube. Our appreciation statements need to remain free of comparisons with other students, judgments, and criticism related to other behaviors.

Give Written Words of Appreciation

Appreciation can be written as well as verbal. Students have been known to cherish notes of appreciation from teachers for great lengths of time. I'll never forget being told by a parent that her daughter had tacked above her desk in the college dorm an appreciation note I'd written her years ago.

We can write words of appreciation directly on students' papers, or we can use "happygrams." Happygrams are colorful sheets with catchy headings like "Something to Crow About," on which we can write a few words of appreciation or a positive I-message. We can purchase happygrams commercially or make our own.

Teach Students to Ask for Appreciation

Since we can't see and comment on every positive thing that happens in the classroom, we can ask students to let us know when they deserve appreciation. Try this experiment:

Put a box of assorted happygrams in the back of the room, and invite students to write notes of appreciation to themselves about their own behavior. At the end of the day, have them read their notes to you. If you think the notes are accurate, sign them and encourage students to take them home.

This activity is a great exercise in building self-esteem because it enables students to learn how to appreciate themselves by noticing their own positive behavior.

Affirmation

To acknowledge a student's positive personality traits, we can make a verbal or written affirmation statement. Since traits are intangible and cannot be captured on film, they are best recognized via statements about the doer rather than the

Let students share their happygrams with you or each other.

deed. Affirmation statements encourage students to believe in their known desirable traits and to become aware of hidden traits. When their positive traits are recognized, students feel good not only about themselves but also about us because we took the time to notice and comment.

The more vivid, specific, and enthusiastic our language, the greater the impact of our affirmation statement on a student. Here are some positive traits that we can acknowledge verbally or in writing:

ambition	*fairness*	*patience*
bravery	*friendliness*	*persistence*
cheerfulness	*gentleness*	*politeness*
cleanliness	*good intentions*	*popularity*
cleverness	*graciousness*	*punctuality*
consideration	*helpfulness*	*risk-taking*
courage	*honesty*	*sensitivity*
creativity	*humility*	*seriousness*
curiosity	*intelligence*	*strength*
dedication	*kindness*	*talent*
dependability	*loyalty*	*thoughtfulness*
effort	*neatness*	*truthfulness*
energy	*organization*	*understanding*
enthusiasm	*originality*	*wit*

Making such statements as "I acknowledge your kindness" or "Wow! What creativity!" may seem strange at first. But once we see the wonderful effect of such statements on our students, we will quickly begin using them naturally.

Affection

In *The Whole Child,* Joanne Hendrick says, "An aura of happiness and affection . . . [establishes] that basic feeling of well-being which is essential to successful learning."[2] Good teachers are those who not only can present information in a coherent, intelligent manner but also can establish mutually affectionate and rewarding relationships with their students.

Affection Breeds Affection

Affection is not a tool to be used to induce or reinforce a particular behavior; rather, it is a gift given with no strings attached. It is not "I like you when . . ." or "I'd like you if . . ." Instead, it is simply "I like you because I like you!" Affection is always addressed to the doer, regardless of the deed. The message that students need to receive from us is this: "I'm likable no matter what. My teacher won't stop liking me if I make a mistake or get into trouble. My teacher likes me because I'm me!"

Affection is often most needed when things go badly. For example, consider this teacher's comments to a student who has failed a test: "Moya, I guess this last test just didn't go well for you. We all make mistakes, though, and maybe the next test will go better. Why don't we have lunch together today so we can talk some more?"

Such comments go a long way toward establishing a rewarding friendship with the student. Had the teacher pointed out to Moya that her inattention during lectures probably caused her to fail the test, Moya probably would have responded with resentment, and the situation might have worsened. The teacher's act of kindness—the lunch invitation—helps Moya understand that the teacher really respects her and cares about her.

Acts of kindness toward students can multiply astronomically. A colleague of mine used to draw out students in a pensive mood by handing them a penny and saying, "Penny for your thoughts." One day, one of her students came to her and poured out an enormous pile of pennies collected from classmates. Looking up at her earnestly, the student explained, "We didn't want you to run out!"

"What goes around, comes around," the saying goes. This is certainly true of affection. Those who demonstrate that they genuinely like us are hard to resist. Friendships with our students are some of our best assets when we have to discipline. Students are more willing to follow the rules and advice of a friend than those of a foe.

The Affectionate Touch

The value of touch has been well established. We've long known that infants thrive when they are touched and held frequently. This need to be touched stays with most of us all our lives, which makes handshakes, back pats, and hugs very effective ways to show affection.

Valid concerns do exist about the amount and kind of touching appropriate in a school setting. The best guideline is the comfort level of both the teacher and the student. Of particular importance is using common sense and sensitivity in regard to touching students of the opposite sex, especially those in junior and senior high. Young people at these ages are not always in control of their sexual feelings, and a nurturing hug or even a back pat could easily be misconstrued.

We also have to take into account that students who have a lot of power and revenge behaviors generally do not like to be touched by teachers. With these students, we have to stick to verbal forms of affection.

How Many A's Make an A+ Relationship?

The Chapter 15 Chart illustrates how we can verbalize the five A's to give students an internal shot of self-esteem and thereby form A+ relationships with them.

Teachers often ask if overdoing the A's won't result in "spoiled students." Can we give too much attention? Express too much appreciation? Show too much affection? I don't think we ever could spoil students with too many A's; however, we do spoil students in three other ways:

- when we overlook their misbehaviors and don't take appropriate action
- when we do too many things for them that they could do for themselves
- when we bail them out of unpleasant situations that they themselves created

When given appropriately, the A's are always helpful. In fact, we could double, triple, even quadruple the dosage without risking harmful side effects. Increasing the A's is the best response when we perceive that a student is experiencing stress. Whatever the cause of the stress—an illness, a breakup with a boyfriend or girlfriend, a separation or divorce in the family—we can immediately respond by upping the student's intake of "vitamin A's."

One disheartening thing about the A's is that they are difficult to give to the students who need them most. Who feels like appreciating a student who causes no end of trouble day after day? However difficult this may be for us, acting positively toward such a student is crucial to his or her well-being. Once we begin, we'll find it becomes easier and easier to continue, and we'll discover that our boosts to the student's self-esteem will pay off in improved behavior.

Another point to keep in mind about giving out A's is that many young people don't hear positive remarks. They're so used to being criticized and reprimanded that kind words just pass by them. We may need to watch a student's facial expression and body language to make sure we've made an impression. If we haven't, we'll have to repeat what we've said or even ask, "Did you hear what I just said?" Sometimes we have to teach students to be receptive to an A + relationship. Once they begin experiencing the benefits of this new way of relating, however, they will soon become eager participants.

Continue Step 4: Select A's to Help Students Connect

Continue completing Step 4 of the School Action Plan by choosing ways to give A's that will help you and your student connect by forming an A + relationship. The A's, which are summarized in the Chapter 15 Chart, are helpful with all students, but they are particularly beneficial for students with attention-seeking, power, and revenge behaviors. For example, students misbehaving for extra attention will start to change their ways when we help them learn how to ask for attention appropriately. Students with the goal of power or revenge can benefit from extra doses of acceptance and judicious affection.

Like encouragement techniques, the A's are not tied directly to the goal of the student's misbehavior. Recall some of the student's positive behaviors and choose A's that will reinforce those behaviors. After all, you don't want to undo what's going wrong at the expense of ignoring what's going right!

Under Step 4 of the Action Plan, be as specific as possible about each A you've chosen. Note how and when you think you'll give or model the A. The more details you include, the more effective your plan will be.

Remember that under Step 4 you'll also be adding encouragement techniques that help the student *contribute* successfully. These techniques are discussed in Chapter 16.

A summary chart of all the encouragement techniques is presented in Appendix D, The Building Blocks of Self-Esteem.

Notes

1. Barbara Clark, *Growing Up Gifted* (Columbus, Ohio: Merrill, 1979), 154.

2. Joanne Hendrick, *The Whole Child: New Trends in Early Education* (St. Louis: Mosby, 1980), 4.

Five A's to an A+ Relationship

	What the teacher is saying	*What the student is hearing*
Acceptance	You're okay.	I'm okay.
Attention	I see you.	I am important.
Appreciation	Thank you for . . .	My efforts are noticed.
Affirmation	I know something wonderful about you.	I am worthwhile.
Affection	I like you.	Somebody cares about me.

All the above are surefire ways to raise self-esteem.

1 The kind of student that I have the most difficulty accepting is:

_____

_____

2 Sometimes, the praise I give students fails because:

_____

_____

3 When I want to encourage a positive behavior, I would use these A's:

_____

_____

_____

4 I currently give attention to students in these ways:

_____

_____

5 One A I want to give more of in the future is _____.
The reason I want to give this A is because:

_____

_____

Continued on next page.

6 One student in my class who needs more A's is _____
In the next two weeks, I'll try to give this student more A's in these ways:

_____

_____

_____

7 I can teach my students to ask for A's when they feel they need them in these ways:

_____

_____

_____

8 "A teacher can never give too many A's to one student." I agree or disagree with this
statement because:

_____

_____

_____

_____

Helping Students Contribute

As teachers, we want to encourage students to care about and contribute to their class and classmates. When we help students understand that their personal welfare is linked to the welfare of others, we are well on the way to developing responsible, concerned, and involved citizens.

"The need to be needed is often more powerful than the need to survive," states Dr. Stephen Glenn in *Raising Children for Success.* [1] Glenn hypothesizes that depression and suicide result from the perception that one's life has no meaning, no purpose, no significance. When we structure our rooms so that each student is asked to contribute to the welfare of the class and classmates, we satisfy the need to be needed in at least one area of a young person's life.

While we want to give all students opportunities to contribute, we have to make a special effort to help students with avoidance-of-failure behaviors feel needed. These students generally don't feel capable, and, without our help, they don't recognize ways in which they can contribute.

When students contribute, they feel needed. Students who are needed feel they belong. Those who belong develop high self-esteem. Students with high self-esteem have much to contribute. It's a wonderful circular process in which each part reinforces the other.

We can encourage students to contribute by using the techniques described in this chapter. The techniques are grouped according to two strategies.

Satisfying the Need to Be Needed

Strategy 1: Encourage Students' Contributions to the Class

When we give students some responsibility as well as voice and choice in classroom and curriculum matters, we foster critical thinking skills, inspire a sense of ownership, and promote an attitude of willing participation. Asking students to state opinions and preferences involves granting them a certain amount of independence and legitimate power. We've already learned that allowing legitimate power is an essential precaution against the eruption of power struggles in the classroom.

Invite students' help with daily tasks. One way to enable students to contribute to the welfare of the class is to turn over to them as many of the daily classroom duties as possible. So many of the tasks we spend time on don't require our expertise. For example, students can take attendance, inventory books and supplies, deliver messages, collect lunch money, straighten up the classroom, sort worksheets, alphabetize books, and operate audiovisual equipment.

Students enjoy helping out. They relish being useful. As long as we demonstrate the attitude that "I'm asking you to do this because I know you are capable and I need your help," students see tasks as privileges instead of chores. On the other hand, if we give the impression that we're asking for their help because the task is too menial for us, they'll refuse.

One wise sixth-grade teacher, when making out the beginning-of-the-year task chart, always lists two or three more tasks than there are students in her class. That way she can greet a child entering class later in the year with the delighted exclamation, "I'm sure glad you've come to this class! We really need you. We haven't had enough students to do all the things that need to be done around here." You can bet that a new student feels instantly connected and valued in her classroom.

Request students' curriculum choices. Another way that students can contribute to the welfare of the class is to express their opinions and preferences concerning the curriculum, especially in secondary schools. Often we can present students with choices about when, how, and even where a certain subject or lesson should be conducted. For example, the tenth-grade curriculum at Harbor High may call for students to read one of Shakespeare's plays. Students in Mr. Grundy's class might choose to read the play before spring break, while students in Ms. Peachum's class may want to begin after the break. Mr. Grundy's students might prefer assigning parts and reading the play aloud, while Ms. Peachum's group may want to use various video and audio recordings. Mr. Grundy's class may choose to write one long paper, while Ms. Peachum's students may decide to write several short essays. Allowing students this kind of autonomy gives them a vested interest in actively participating in the class, and it may give us a fresh perspective on material we've been teaching for years.

Older students can also choose learning goals, write learning contracts, decide which resources to use, and carry out in-depth courses of study quite independently.

Even first graders can make some simple curriculum and procedural choices: Should we sit at desks during reading group, or should we sit in a circle on a rug in the corner of the room? Should we record each person reading a sentence out loud? How should our worksheets be done today, in pencil or crayon?

Ask students' input for rules. Rules should not be established to make students behave. The real purpose of rules is to help teachers teach effectively, to help students learn effectively, and to help the class function effectively. If we shift our focus from "Follow the rules because I say so" to "Follow the rules because you'll reap important benefits," our students will become more cooperative.

When students disobey rules, teachers commonly say, "You forgot the rule!" In my opinion, students rarely *forget* a rule. Rather they *choose to ignore* the rule, knowing full well that their behavior is inappropriate. We can repeat rules over and over, hoping students will finally remember them, but this won't stop students from choosing to ignore rules. A way to encourage students to "remember" the rules is to invite students to aid in creating them.

Students can assist in creating two types of rules—"helps" and "sabs." Helps include all the things that make classroom learning easy and successful. Sabs include things that sabotage learning and make life difficult. We can ask students, "What behaviors help you get what you want out of this class? What behaviors keep you from succeeding?" Using their responses, we can compile a list of helps and sabs to serve as classroom guidelines.

Frequent modifications of helps and sabs keep the students involved in remembering the rules. They need to continue thinking about how their behavior affects their learning and contributes to the general classroom atmosphere.

Strategy 2: Encourage Students to Help Other Students

When students help one another, their self-esteem rises. They are able not only to make a significant contribution to the class but also to establish a special connection with classmates.

Peer tutoring. Tutoring is one way in which students can help each other. If a student is having trouble with a geometry theorem that we've just explained for the third time, chances are that another student's explanation will make more sense than our fourth try. A struggling student's anxiety level is often lessened when a peer presents the information, and students do seem to speak a special language of their own, unknown to any teacher. In any class, we can usually find many potential pupil professors who are willing to assist classmates.

Peer tutoring helps the tutor as much as the tutee. Recall the saying "You don't really know a subject until you teach it to someone else." When Ali has to explain the use of coordinates on a map to another child, he first must clarify his own understanding and perfect his own skills.

Students in every grade can get involved in peer tutoring. Seventh graders can help other seventh graders with social studies, or fifth graders can help first graders with reading skills. High school math whizzes can help students at all grade levels with math. I've even seen eight-year-old "computerniks" show high schoolers how to write simple programs.

Peer tutoring can be done on an informal or formal basis. Two classes might pair up so students can help one another. A secondary school could take on the project of helping students in a nearby elementary school. At the very least, a classroom could have a sign-up chart entitled "Skills I'm Willing to Teach Others."

Every student is capable of making a contribution when peer tutoring occurs in nonacademic areas. I remember Marcia, a sixth grader at least three years behind in basic skills, who volunteered to teach jumping rope. First graders with poor motor coordination thoroughly enjoyed working with Marcia to master this skill. In turn, Marcia's self-esteem was enhanced. For children who exhibit

"Appreciation Password" can help students build better relationships.

avoidance-of-failure behaviors, nonacademic tutoring provides a way to make much-needed connections with other students and to savor a taste of success.

Peer counseling. Another way that students can contribute to the welfare of classmates is through adult-supervised peer counseling programs. Many secondary schools have established such programs in which students work with peers experiencing difficulty in some aspect of their life. Peer counseling is done one-to-one or in small groups.

As with peer tutoring, peer counseling helps the counselor as much as the counselee. The training that student counselors receive in communication skills and in personal development issues is invaluable. The experience of being able to help a classmate overcome a difficulty also provides a real boost to self-esteem.

Peer recognition. A third way we can enable students to help one another is through peer recognition activities. These are several effective techniques:

- **Applause:** We can encourage students to applaud one another's achievements (Chapter 14).

- **Appreciation and Affirmation Statements:** We can teach students how to make effective appreciation statements to one another and how to affirm one another's positive traits (Chapter 15).

- **Happygrams:** Students can write happygrams that contain appreciation statements to one another (Chapter 15).

- **Appreciation Password:** Each student can be asked to say a few words of appreciation to another student before leaving the room for lunch or another class. This is a variation of Classroom Password, which is described in Chapter 14.

Complete Step 4: Select Encouragement Techniques to Help Students Contribute

Complete Step 4 of your School Action Plan by choosing several techniques that will help your student feel needed by making contributions to the class and to classmates. Many of these techniques, which are summarized in the Chapter 16 Chart, involve total class participation, thereby giving your Action Plan student the opportunity to connect with the group in a responsible and concerned way.

For students who fear failure, making contributions can be a means of recognizing feelings of capability. By helping them discover how to make contributions in nonacademic areas such as helping with classroom tasks, we can give them a taste of feeling capable and then encourage them to achieve the same sensation in their schoolwork. Students with the goal of power can find that having a choice in curriculum and a voice in creating rules provides a positive outlet for their urge to control. Those students seeking revenge can discover that their need to lash out lessens when they're involved in contributing to their own welfare and that of their usual targets—us and classmates. Attention seekers can channel their enormous need to connect into positive ways when we ask them to help us with classroom tasks or to assist classmates in academic and nonacademic areas.

Under Step 4 of the Action Plan, be as specific as possible about each "contributing" technique you've chosen. Note how and when you think you'll use the technique. The more details you include, the more effective your plan will be.

A summary chart of all the encouragement techniques is presented in Appendix D, The Building Blocks of Self-Esteem.

Note

1. Stephen Glenn with Jane Nelsen, *Raising Children for Success* (Fair Oaks, Calif.: Sunrise Press, 1987), 87. Also available in an edition entitled *Raising Self-Reliant Children in a Self-Indulgent World,* Pima Press.

Helping Students Contribute

General Strategy	Techniques
Encourage students' contributions to the class.	Invite students' help with daily tasks.
	Request students' curriculum choices.
	Ask students' input for rules.
Encourage students to help other students.	Peer tutoring.
	Peer counseling.
	Peer recognition:
	Applause.
	Appreciation and affirmation statements.
	Happygrams.
	Appreciation password.

1 Inviting students to participate in the daily routine and to make curriculum choices is important because:

_____

_____

2 Some ways that I currently invite students to participate in the daily routine are:

_____

_____

_____

3 Some new ways that I can invite students to participate in the daily routine are:

_____

_____

_____

4 Some ways that I currently invite students to participate in making curriculum choices are:

_____

_____

_____

5 Some new ways that I can invite students to participate in making curriculum choices are:

_____

_____

_____

Continued on next page.

6 Do my students participate in creating rules? _____ Why or why not?

_____

_____

7 Some of the ways that my students help each other are:

_____

_____

_____

8 Some new ways in which I could encourage my students to help each other are:

_____

_____

_____

7

SECTION SEVEN

Taking Cooperative Action

The *Cooperative Discipline* program sets up a realistic parent-teacher partnership. Parents cannot directly alleviate discipline problems that occur in school any more than teachers can control discipline matters at home. We therefore ask parents to work on discipline problems on the home front, while we work on those that occur during the school day. Together, we cooperate to set up intervention and encouragement techniques. When parents and teachers, the most significant adults in a young person's life, establish common goals and use compatible strategies, the *Cooperative Discipline* process is underway.

CHAPTER 17
Cooperative Discipline as a Cooperative Effort

Parents play a vital role in the *Cooperative Discipline* process. We need them to help boost their child's self-esteem. We need them to help teach their child that misbehaving for attention, power, revenge, or to avoid failure doesn't pay off. When parents and teachers, the most significant adults in a young person's life, establish common goals and use compatible strategies, the *Cooperative Discipline* process is underway.

The *Cooperative Discipline* program sets up a realistic parent-teacher partnership. Parents cannot directly alleviate discipline problems that occur in school any more than teachers can control discipline matters at home; long-distance discipline doesn't work. We therefore ask parents to work on discipline problems at home, while we work on those that occur during the school day. Together, we cooperate to set up intervention and encouragement techniques appropriate for both home and school. Young people, of course, benefit from experiencing the same approach in both places.

Discipline problems in school frequently mirror discipline problems in the home, for the same forces that work against effective discipline procedures at school usually work against them at home. To help parents recognize these shared problems and to convince them to become our partners in the discipline process, we need to offer them information about effective intervention and encouragement strategies to use at home. This is not really a new role for us. In most parent-teacher conferences concerning misbehaving students, we probably request parents to do certain things at home to help their children behave better in school. In using the *Cooperative Discipline* program, we simply become more efficient and effective providers of parent education. The program enables us to teach parents a variety of strategies that mirror and reinforce those we're using in the classroom.

Convincing parents to become our partners in the discipline process is usually not a hard sell. In many communities, parents view school personnel as the most approachable, and perhaps the only, source of guidance for dealing with misbehavior. Moreover, parents often think that if they seek help from sources that offer therapy, such as community mental health centers, they will be considered failures by friends and family. Approaching educators for information on problems with misbehaving children seems far less threatening.

It's no secret that young people from homes with effective intervention and encouragement strategies cause less difficulty in school than those from homes with lax or ineffective discipline. So any work we do to educate parents directly benefits us as well as our students. We may even discover that as parent effectiveness improves, student achievement scores go up. A team of researchers headed by Sanford M. Dornbusch at Stanford University Center for the Study of Families, Children, and Youth found that a link exists between parenting styles and children's academic performance.[1] The cooperative style correlates with the highest grades, whereas both autocratic and permissive parenting styles are associated with lower grades.

Educating parents about effective discipline is not as difficult a job as we might think, particularly since the theoretical framework of *Cooperative Discipline* is translated into the School Action Plan. The School Action Plan provides a format for discussion, enabling us to share information and concerns with parents, and it can also serve as a model for parents interested in preparing a Home Action Plan. Parents, like teachers, need to understand the four goals of misbehavior since misbehavior at home, as well as at school, is usually directed toward one of these goals. Parents, like teachers, need to know appropriate intervention strategies to counteract misbehavior, and encouragement strategies to boost self-esteem.

Informing Parents About Cooperative Discipline

The best time to inform parents about the *Cooperative Discipline* program is *before* any problems occur. In this way, we greatly increase the chances of a supportive response rather than a defensive reaction from parents if we do experience difficulties with their child. When parents understand what the *Cooperative Discipline* process involves—interventions as well as encouragement strategies—they usually become willing partners, backing our efforts in the classroom and receptive to our suggestions about what reinforcement steps may be taken at home.

Written policy statement. We can initially inform parents about the *Cooperative Discipline* program via a written policy statement. Such a policy statement could be in the form of a photocopied handout, a printed booklet, or a section in the school handbook.

A policy statement for *Cooperative Discipline* would include a general description of the program's philosophy, a brief explanation of the four goals of misbehavior, a list of the intervention strategies, a summary of the ways to build self-esteem through encouragement, and perhaps a blank copy of the School Action Plan. The statement also might suggest ways in which parents could establish an encouraging home atmosphere that would inspire a successful school experience.

Newsletter column. Regularly distributed parent newsletters could include a column entitled "The Discipline Corner," which discusses specific interventions and encouragement strategies within the *Cooperative Discipline* process. In this way, parents are kept informed about efforts being made to improve student behavior.

Parent group presentation. At least one PTA, PTO, or parents' meeting each year ought to concern the *Cooperative Discipline* process and how parents can assist the process through encouragement at home. Such a meeting would also provide parents with the opportunity to react to the program and to ask questions.

Parent resource library. The school librarian can establish a section entitled "Cooperative Discipline Resources for Parents," which contains books, audiotapes, and videotapes that parents can use in developing discipline strategies compatible with those used by teachers. Suggested resources are listed in Appendix G, Parent Resource Library.

Parents can be informed about these resources through fliers, newsletters, or announcements at PTA or PTO meetings. Short reviews of the material, written by parents, could be included in the school newsletter.

Parent drop-in center. Parent resource material can be available in a special room at school where parents can drop in for a cup of coffee and browse through the information. At specific times, a teacher, counselor, school psychologist, social worker, or administrator could be on hand to discuss parental concerns about discipline at home or school.

Parent study groups. Schools can offer parent training programs that are conducted by school counselors, psychologists, administrators, classroom teachers, or knowledgeable parents. Programs that are consistent with *Cooperative Discipline*'s theory are listed in Appendix H, Parent Training Programs. These programs have extensive leader's guides and teaching materials so that the group leader needn't be a parenting professional.

Establishing an Atmosphere of Mutual Support

It's up to us to ensure that phone calls and conferences inspire parental cooperation instead of defensive hostility. To encourage positive responses, we can keep these guidelines in mind:

Talk about misbehavior in objective terms. Parents may become overwhelmed by subjective, judgmental labels. For example, parents hearing the statement that "Winona is almost constantly disruptive" are more likely to react defensively than if they are told that "Winona calls out answers without raising her hand about five times a day."

Limit the complaints to three or four specific misbehaviors. Mentioning every transgression that a student has ever committed will stagger even the most cooperative of parents. If we give just a few choice examples of the misbehavior causing the most concern, parents can grasp what's going on without being deluged by bad news.

Avoid predicting future failures. "Mr. and Mrs. Palermo, if your daughter Juliette doesn't stop this behavior soon, she'll never get a high school diploma." For parents, just hearing how their child is behaving today is usually enough to bear, without the added worry about what the child might or might not be doing a year from now.

Anticipate success. We want to avoid giving parents the impression that we consider their child to be incorrigible. If we throw up our hands and sigh, "I don't know what to do with your child," parents will lose confidence in us, in themselves, and in their child. A better approach is to show parents that we've thought a great deal about their child by presenting a specific plan—a School Action Plan. If we also mention some positive behaviors and predict success, we are usually rewarded with favorable parental responses.

Don't take defensive reactions personally. When we hear upsetting news, a defensive response is natural. When children cause problems in school, parents often react defensively to cover up how they actually feel—guilty, powerless, fearful, and overwhelmed. Let's take a closer look at each of these feelings, for when we understand how parents feel, we're better able to respond empathetically.

Guilty—Since many parents believe that behavior is caused rather than chosen, they blame themselves for not being good enough parents.

Powerless—Parents think they are supposed to know how to make their children behave, both at home and at school. When parents realize that their discipline efforts aren't working, they wind up feeling powerless.

Fearful—When teachers describe today's problems, many parents are gnawed by fears about the future. "If my six-year-old is disturbing others and not paying attention in first grade, what will happen when he gets to junior high?" "If my fifteen-year-old is not handing in assignments and is cutting classes today, will she drop out and end up on the streets next year?"

Overwhelmed—Balancing home and career isn't easy, especially for a single parent. Many parents work outside the home during the day and attempt to fulfill all their parenting and housekeeping duties during evenings and weekends. When we tell already overwhelmed parents about their child's classroom problems, we could be adding the straw that breaks the camel's back.

Don't ask for the impossible. Sometimes parents get impossible requests from teachers. "Mrs. MacDougall, please talk to Scottie and make sure he doesn't come to class late any more." "Mr. Capistrant, impress upon Carlos that his attitude and work habits must improve if he's to pass algebra this year." When parents receive requests like these, they may feel justifiably upset, for they may not know how to accomplish such tasks. The consequences for inappropriate behavior in school need to be established and enforced by the teacher, not by the parents. Long-distance discipline doesn't work. Parents cannot directly alleviate discipline problems that occur in school any more than teachers can moderate discipline problems in the student's home. Therefore, any requests made of parents are best described in the form of specific actions that can be taken at home.

Notifying Parents About Their Child's School Action Plan

When we're having sufficient difficulty with a student to warrant developing a School Action Plan, we need to notify the parents and to share the plan with them.

Initial phone call to parents. The first step, whenever possible, is making a phone call to parents to let them know that a problem exists. This personal contact can help us form a congenial relationship with the parents.

If we've already informed parents about the *Cooperative Discipline* program, they'll know that a School Action Plan is formulated when a student misbehaves. During the phone call, we can remind parents about the plan and offer two options: either we'll send home a copy of the completed plan, or we'll set up a conference with the parents to discuss the plan and to explore the possible development of a Home Action Plan to support the efforts being made at school.

Second phone call to parents. If parents do not wish a conference, we send home a copy of the School Action Plan with Steps 1 to 4 completed, and then follow up with a second phone call a few days later. At this point, we can answer parents' questions about the plan and gain their input concerning the selected intervention and encouragement techniques. We also can remind parents that the school is willing to help them formulate a Home Action Plan modeled on the School Action Plan. Under Step 5 of the School Action Plan, we can indicate that we've shared the plan with the parents and note any efforts they're willing to make at home to redirect their child's behavior. After twenty years of working with parents, I have found that most are open to suggestions, especially on how to build self-esteem.

Structuring the Parent-Teacher Conference

When parents agree to join us for a conference regarding their child's misbehavior, we can structure the conference according to the steps in the School Action Plan. Reviewing the steps of the plan with parents gives us the opportunity to explain firsthand the concepts and procedures of the *Cooperative Discipline* program.

Prior to the conference, we need to complete Steps 1 through 4 of the plan. With the plan in hand, we can then explain to the parents exactly what misbehavior we've observed, the goal of the misbehavior, and the intervention and encouragement strategies we've selected. Sometimes, we'll have strong preferences concerning which intervention and encouragement strategies to use; other times, we may want to ask parents for additional suggestions. Parents often have helpful insights about what works with their child, and when they can help make the decisions, they gain not only an understanding of the *Cooperative Discipline* strategies but also confidence in the School Action Plan.

After discussing Steps 1 through 4 of the plan with parents, we can undertake Step 5 by requesting that parents continue to participate in the *Cooperative Discipline* process as our partners. They may choose to become silent partners, who receive periodic reports about their child's progress, or they may want to become active partners, eager to devise a Home Action Plan that will reinforce the School Action Plan and alleviate behavior problems at home. Procedures for developing a Home Action Plan are discussed later in this chapter.

What if parents reject any involvement in the School Action Plan? Although our job will be more difficult without parental interest or partnership, we still can achieve some results single-handedly.

Young people don't necessarily expect all adults to react the same when they misbehave. What works with Mom won't always work with Dad, and what works with Dad won't always work with Teacher. If we use sound classroom discipline procedures and follow through carefully on intervention and encouragement strategies, we can at least make a difference when the student is with us. In some cases, we'll have to settle for that.

Structuring the Parent-Teacher-Student Conference

When we invite the student to join us and parents to discuss a School Action Plan, we are putting some of the responsibility for solving behavior problems where it belongs—on the student. Since a School Action Plan is intended to help the student choose more appropriate behavior, the student's insight about the problem and possible solutions can be invaluable. Moreover, when the student realizes that *both* parents and teacher are determined to end the misbehavior, he or she usually begins to understand that it's time to make a change.

Before involving the student in the conference, we first may want to meet privately with the parents to exchange information. For instance, we could discuss Steps 1 and 2 of the School Action Plan alone with parents. Then we could invite the student to join parents and us in reviewing and formulating the plan, following these guidelines:

Describe misbehaviors objectively. The student portion of the conference begins with an accurate description of the misbehaviors that are causing difficulty at school. The more objective and nonjudgmental our words, the more cooperation we'll win from the student. Evaluative language will only make the student defensive, getting the conference off to a bad start. Identifying the goal of the misbehavior is unnecessary, since this step is primarily a means for us to identify appropriate types of interventions.

Focus on the future. Discussions about the past need to be avoided during the conference. Searches for causes of the misbehavior or student excuses for the misbehavior aren't helpful, since the past can't be changed. The focus needs to be on the future, on preventing the misbehavior from recurring. We can cut off any digressions by insisting, "Let's talk only about what we can do so that the behavior doesn't happen again."

Discuss intervention strategies. After the behavior has been described, the various intervention strategies are discussed. When dealing with power or revenge behavior, we talk with the student only about the resolution stage—devising consequences. When dealing with avoidance-of-failure behavior, we share with the student the ways we can modify the curriculum, use different instructional methods, provide tutoring, or teach self-talk. When dealing with attention-seeking behavior, we skip any talk about intervention strategies and immediately discuss encouragement techniques and appropriate ways to ask for attention. Any talk about interventions only gives these students the extra attention they desire, which is the payoff we're trying to prevent.

Set consequences. If we can negotiate a solution or determine consequences that everyone agrees would be best, fine. If the student balks at all suggestions and stonewalls the conversation, we can make the decision without the student: "Since you aren't willing to choose right now, the rest of us are going to decide what action to take." Unworkable solutions suggested by the student need not be accepted. We have the ultimate authority over what happens in school and, therefore, the right to insist on a sensible solution.

Discuss encouragement strategies. After we've completed the School Action Plan through Step 3, we prepare for Step 4 by gathering information from the student. We ask, "What can we do to make the classroom, home, or both a better place for you?" We try to see through the student's eyes, to know what makes him or her feel a sense of belonging, and what doesn't. After gathering this information from the student, appropriate encouragement strategies for home and school can be chosen.

Seek continuing parental involvement. When Step 4 has been completed, the student can be excused from the conference, and we can then discuss Step 5

Some young people are real pros at playing school against home.

with parents—their continuing involvement as partners in the plan. At this time, they may choose to develop a Home Action Plan.

Plan a follow-up conference. A follow-up conference with parents needn't be long, just enough time to make any necessary changes to the School Action Plan, Home Action Plan, or both.

Students from nursery school on up can be involved in conferences. Of course, the younger the student, the smaller the role. For a preschool or primary student, involvement is only really necessary for power or revenge behavior. Such a young student can be given the choice between two consequences selected ahead of time by the teacher and parents. On the other hand, high school students can have a greater say in negotiating solutions and choosing consequences. The more they have their say, the more cooperative and responsible they'll act and feel.

Developing a Home Action Plan

Once a School Action Plan has been completed, it's time to talk about the possibility of preparing a Home Action Plan. The question to ask parents is, "At home, do you see behavior similar to what I see in school?" The answer could be "Yes" or "No."

Because of the differences in environment between home and school, a student may have learned how to appropriately connect, contribute, and feel capable in one setting but not in the other. If the parents don't think that there are similar discipline problems to be worked on at home, then we can concentrate on helping them plan some encouragement strategies that they can use to boost their child's self-esteem. The higher the child's self-esteem, the easier it will be to correct misbehavior in the classroom.

More likely than not, however, parents will admit that they are bothered at home by behaviors similar to those we've observed in the classroom. When this is the case, we can suggest helping the parents write a Home Action Plan similar to that prepared for school.

We can help parents develop a four-step Home Action Plan by following the procedures used in constructing a School Action Plan. We can also include the student in the process by means of a parent-teacher-student conference. These are the steps followed in preparing a Home Action Plan:

Step 1: Pinpoint and Describe the Child's Behavior

Nonspecific, judgmental words like *disrespectful* or *disobedient* won't work. Ask the parents to describe the misbehavior as objectively as possible. Their objective descriptions are written under Step 1 of the plan.

Step 2: Identify the goal of the misbehavior

Use the Review Chart of the Four Goals of Misbehavior (Appendix A) and the Teacher and Student Response Clues to Identifying the Goal of Misbehavior (Appendix B) to help parents determine the goal of the misbehavior occurring at home. This goal is written under Step 2 of the plan.

If more than one goal of misbehavior is identified by the parents, encourage them to work first on attention-seeking or avoidance-of-failure behaviors since these tend to be easier to deal with than power or revenge behaviors. Once parents have experienced some success, they'll be encouraged to tackle the more difficult behaviors.

Step 3: Choose Intervention Techniques for the Moment of Misbehavior

Use the Summary Chart of Interventions (Appendix C) to help parents explore options for handling misbehaviors at home. While we can recommend which interventions to use, parents should make the final choice. Their selected interventions are written under Step 3 of the plan.

Assisting parents in choosing interventions for power or revenge behaviors is probably the most difficult step for us in helping devise a Home Action Plan. This is because the home application of many of the strategies is somewhat different from school. For example, parents can make a "graceful exit" by simply walking out of a room, leaving alone the child who is spouting I-hate-you statements. As teachers, we don't have this option. Likewise, some of the options we may have, such as sending a child to another classroom, are unavailable to parents.

We can brainstorm possible consequences for revenge or power behaviors with the parents, or we can refer parents to a school resource person such as an administrator, counselor, psychologist, or a parent volunteer trained in one of the recommended parent education programs.

Another resource that can help parents in completing Step 3 of the Home Action Plan is *Coping With Kids*.[2] This book outlines specific consequences for use in over 100 different situations.

Step 4: Select Encouragement Techniques to Build Self-Esteem

Talk about various encouragement techniques with parents, but allow them to decide which to include under Step 4 of the plan. The summary chart of encouragement techniques in Appendix D—The Building Blocks of Self-Esteem—is helpful in counseling parents.

After parents have developed a Home Action Plan, set a date for a follow-up in about two weeks. This can be either a phone conversation or a conference during which we can check to see how well the plan is working. Further phone conversations or meetings on a regular basis will allow us to monitor progress and help modify the Home Action Plan as needed.

If the student's behavior begins to improve at home, at school, or in both places, the same intervention strategies can be retained, and perhaps some encouragement techniques can be added to the Home and School Action Plans. The more the student's self-esteem is boosted, the more permanent the change in behavior is likely to be.

If the misbehavior does not abate, we have a number of choices to discuss with parents. When parents take action, misbehavior often gets worse before it gets better, for young people like to test the parental resolve to carry through. Therefore, both we and the parents may want to stick with our respective plans for another week or two before making any changes.

School Support for Parents as Partners

Classroom teachers can't always do it alone. We may need help from others in the school community to support our efforts to enlist parents as partners in the discipline process.

Because of their specialized training, school counselors, psychologists, and social workers can be most helpful in explaining to parents how to apply the *Cooperative Discipline* procedures at home, and in devising intervention and encouragement strategies. As neutral observers not directly involved in any of the interactions that are causing problems, they can provide an invaluable perspective on the misbehavior that's occurring. When they're invited to participate in a conference with teacher, parents, and student, they can use their mediation skills to deal with any misunderstanding or disagreement that may arise among the participants. Since they're trained in understanding emotions, they can help a participant express and cope with strong feelings.

If we're dealing with a student who has sought revenge by destroying school property, we may want to invite a school administrator to join a conference. The administrator's role would be similar to that of a counselor or psychologist—an impartial participant. Moreover, the presence of an administrator, as a representative of the ultimate authority in the school, often impresses the seriousness of the matter at hand on the student better than any verbal admonitions.

When we invite the participation of parents, students, specialists, or administrators in the discipline process, we're on our way to establishing cooperative relationships that can make a difference in our students' behavior in and beyond the classroom.

Notes
1. *Parenting,* December 1987, 16.
2. Linda Albert, *Coping With Kids* (Dutton, 1982; Ballantine, 1984).

CHAPTER 17 CHART
Involving Parents as Partners
in the Cooperative Discipline Process

Before Discipline Problems Occur: Inform parents about Cooperative Discipline.

Written policy statement.
Newsletter column.
Parent group presentation.
Parent resource library.
Parent drop-in center.
Parent study groups.

To Inspire Parental Cooperation: Establish an atmosphere of mutual support.

Talk about misbehavior in objective terms.
Limit the complaints to three or four specific misbehaviors.
Avoid predicting future failures.
Anticipate success.
Don't take defensive reactions personally.
Don't ask for the impossible.

To Inform Parents Initially About a School Action Plan: Notify parents by phone.

Offer parents two options:

Send home a copy of their child's School Action Plan, and then follow up with a second call to discuss the plan.

Set up a conference to discuss the School Action Plan and perhaps to develop a Home Action Plan.

Follow up with second phone call, if necessary.

Continued on next page.

Conference Options

Parent-Teacher Conference

Review the completed School Action Plan with parents.

Ask parents for their insights concerning interventions and encouragement strategies.

Ask parents to continue as partners in the *Cooperative Discipline* process:

By receiving periodic reports about child's progress.

By devising a Home Action Plan to reinforce the School Action Plan.

Parent-Teacher-Student Conference

First, meet privately with parents to discuss Steps 1 and 2 of the School Action Plan. Involve other school personnel, if necessary.

Invite student to participate in conference, following these steps:

Describe misbehaviors objectively.

Focus on the future.

Discuss intervention strategies.

Set consequences.

Discuss encouragement strategies.

Discuss how parents may want to continue involvement as partners in the *Cooperative Discipline* process:

By receiving periodic reports about child's progress.

By devising a Home Action Plan to reinforce the School Action Plan.

Plan a follow-up conference.

The Home Action Plan

Steps in helping parents develop a Home Action Plan:

Ask parents to pinpoint and describe their child's misbehavior at home.

Help parents identify goal of the misbehavior, using Appendixes A and B.

Help parents and students choose intervention techniques, using Appendix C.

Help parents and students select encouragement techniques, using Appendix D.

1 Why do I need to establish common goals and compatible strategies with parents?

_____

_____

2 What do I view as the task of a parent educator?

_____

_____

3 How will I benefit if parents become more adept at discipline in the home?

_____

_____

4 I believe I am qualified or not qualified to advise parents on how to handle their children at home because:

_____

_____

5 What determines whether I or a parent should be responsible for a given misbehavior?

_____

_____

6 Do I involve students in conferences with parents? Why or why not?

_____

_____

Continued on next page.

7 How am I doing in establishing an atmosphere of mutual support? (On the continuum below, mark where you think you are now):

I talk about behavior only
in objective terms.

I talk about behavior
in subjective terms.

←————————————————————————→

I limit the list of complaints to
three or four specific misbehaviors.

I tell parents everything
a child is doing wrong.

←————————————————————————→

I avoid making predictions about the
future.

I warn parents about the future.

←————————————————————————→

I anticipate success, always noting
positive behaviors.

I give the impression that the
situation is out of control.

←————————————————————————→

I never take defensive reactions personally.

I take defensive reactions personally.

←————————————————————————→

8 How can other school personnel provide support for me if I take on the role of parent educator?

_____

_____

CONCLUSION
Cooperative Discipline in Perspective

Implementing the *Cooperative Discipline* process is the first—and most crucial—step that we can take toward solving discipline problems. Once the process is underway, we can then magnify its influence by fostering a cooperative attitude, both in the classroom and in the total school. Five guidelines can help us achieve this goal in relationship with the *Cooperative Discipline* intervention and encouragement strategies, as illustrated in this section. Here are descriptions of these guidelines:

1. ***Establish a positive school environment.*** All school personnel, from principal to bus driver to maintenance worker, strive to connect with students by building A+ relationships. The school building, as well as each room within it, is pleasantly designed, decorated, and maintained as an inviting place to spend the day.

2. ***Use democratic procedures and policies.*** Students are invited to contribute in meaningful ways to the development and implementation of policies that govern everyday life at school. The primary democratic procedures and policies are class discussions, class councils, and schoolwide student councils.

3. ***Implement cooperative learning strategies.*** Competition can be eliminated from the classroom when students are divided into learning groups. The students in each group develop a sense of personal and communal responsibility as they work together to achieve specific academic goals.

4. ***Conduct classroom guidance activities.*** Such activities focus on helping students understand themselves and others and on teaching students to solve interpersonal problems peaceably by using conflict-resolution skills. Armed with this information, students are better able to develop and mature both individually and socially.

5. ***Choose appropriate curriculum methods and materials.*** Students who are bored because a lesson is too easy or frustrated because a lesson is too hard are likely candidates for misbehavior. Curriculum evaluation should be an ongoing process that considers the needs of all students.

The Cooperative Discipline Program in Perspective

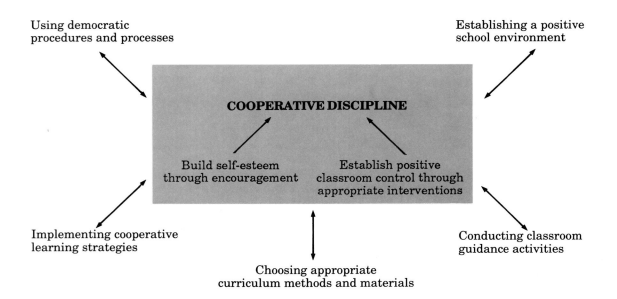

Using democratic
procedures and processes

Establishing a positive
school environment

COOPERATIVE DISCIPLINE

Build self-esteem
through encouragement

Establish positive
classroom control through
appropriate interventions

Implementing cooperative
learning strategies

Conducting classroom
guidance activities

Choosing appropriate
curriculum methods and materials

A Fond Farewell

As we reach the end of our journey together, I wish that meeting each one of you could be a possibility. The road to helping our students become the best they can be is often long, twisted, and frustrating. With the map provided by *Cooperative Discipline*, however, your way has been well marked by practical and positive guidelines. By maintaining confidence and consistency, you're sure to help your students grow in self-esteem and choose appropriate behavior that lasts.

Bibliography

Albert, Linda. *Coping with Kids*. New York: Dutton, 1982; Ballantine, 1984.

——— . *Coping with Kids and School*. New York: Dutton, 1984; Ballantine, 1985.

Albert, Linda, and Michael Popkin. *Quality Parenting*. New York: Random House, 1987; Ballantine, 1989.

Baruth, Leroy, and Daniel Eckstein. *The ABC's of Classroom Discipline*. Dubuque, Iowa: Kendall/Hunt, 1982.

Blessington, John. *Let My Children Work*. Garden City, N.J.: Anchor Books, 1975.

Carlson, Jon, and Casey Thorpe. *The Growing Teacher*. Englewood Cliffs, N.J.: Prentice Hall, 1984.

Charles, C. M. *Building Classroom Discipline*. New York: Longman, 1981.

Dinkmeyer, Don, and Lewis Lonsoncy. *The Encouragement Book*. Englewood Cliffs, N.J.: Prentice Hall, 1980.

Dinkmeyer, Don, Sr., Gary D. McKay, and Don Dinkmeyer, Jr. *Systematic Training for Effective Teaching (STET)*. Circle Pines, Minn.: American Guidance Service, 1980.

Dreikurs, Rudolf. *Psychology in the Classroom*. New York: Harper & Row, 1957, 1968.

Dreikurs, Rudolf, Bernice Bronia Grunwald, and Floy C. Pepper. *Maintaining Sanity in the Classroom*. New York: Harper & Row, 1971, 1982.

Dubelle, Stanley, Jr., and Carol Hoffman. *Misbehavin': Solving the Disciplinary Puzzle for Educators*. Lancaster, Pa.: Technomic Publishing Co., 1984.

——— . *Misbehavin' II*. Lancaster, Pa.: Technomic Publishing Co., 1986.

Ginott, Chaim G. *Teacher and Child: A Book for Parents and Teachers*. New York: Avon Books, 1972.

Glenn, Stephen, with Jane Nelsen. *Raising Children for Success*. Fair Oaks, Calif.: Sunrise Press, 1987.

Glasser, William. *Schools Without Failure*. New York: Harper & Row, 1969.

——— . *Control Theory in the Classroom*. New York: Harper & Row, 1986.

Henderson, Anne, Carl Marburger, and Theodora Ooms. *Beyond the Bake Sale: An Educator's Guide to Working with Parents*. Columbia, Md.: The National Committee for Citizens in Education, 1986.

Hillman, Bill. *Teaching with Confidence*. Springfield, Ill.: Thomas, 1981.

Kreidler, William J. *Creative Conflict Resolution*. Glenview, Ill.: Scott, Foresman, 1984.

LePage, Andy. *Transforming Education*. Oakland, Calif.: Oakmore Press, 1987.

Martin, Robert. *Teaching Through Encouragement*. Englewood Cliffs, N.J.: Prentice Hall, 1980.

Nelsen, Jane. *Positive Discipline*. New York: Ballantine, 1987.

Purkey, William. *Self-Concept and School Achievement*. Englewood Cliffs, N.J.: Prentice Hall, 1970.

Purkey, William, and John Novak. *Inviting School Success*. Belmont, Calif.: Wadsworth, 1978.

Reasoner, Robert W. *Building Self-Esteem*. Palo Alto, Calif.: Consulting Psychologists Press, 1986.

Weiner, Bernard. "Principles for a Theory of Student Motivation and Their Application Within an Attributional Framework," in *Research on Motivation in Education: Student Motivation*, Volume I, eds. R. E. Ames and C. Ames. New York: Academic Press, 1984.

Wilson, John H. *The Invitational Elementary Classroom*. Springfield, Ill.: Charles C. Thomas, 1986.

Review Chart of the Four Goals of Misbehavior

	Attention-Seeking Behavior	Power Behavior
Active Characteristics	*Active AGMs:* Student does all kinds of behaviors that distract teacher and classmates.	*Temper tantrums and verbal tantrums:* Student is disruptive and confrontational.
Passive Characteristics	*Passive AGMs:* Student exhibits one-pea-at-a-time behavior, operates on slow, slower, slowest speeds.	*Quiet noncompliance:* Student does his or her own thing, yet often is pleasant and even agreeable.
Origins of Behavior	Parents and teachers tend to pay more attention to misbehavior than to appropriate behavior. Children aren't taught how to ask for attention appropriately. Children may be deprived of sufficient personal attention.	Changes in society that stress equality in relationships, rather than dominant-submissive roles. The exaltation of the individual and the emphasis on achieving personal power, as epitomized by the human potential movement.
Silver Lining	Student wants a relationship with the teacher (and classmates).	Student exhibits leadership potential, assertiveness, and independent thinking.
Principles of Prevention	Give lots of attention for appropriate behavior. Teach student to ask directly for extra attention when needed.	Avoid and defuse direct confrontations. Grant student legitimate power.
Intervention Strategies*	Minimize the attention. Legitimize the behavior. Do the unexpected. Distract the student. Notice appropriate behavior. Move the student.	Make a graceful exit. Use time-out. Set the consequences.

*For additional information on intervention strategies, see Appendix C.

Revenge Behavior	Avoidance-of-Failure Behavior
Physical and psychological attacks: Student is hurtful to teacher, classmates, or both.	*Frustration tantrum:* Student loses control when the pressure to succeed becomes too intense.
Student is sullen and withdrawn, refusing overtures of friendship.	Student procrastinates, fails to complete projects, develops temporary incapacity, or assumes behaviors that resemble a learning disability.
A reflection of the increasing violence in society. Media role models that solve conflicts by force.	Rule of the red pencil. Unreasonable expectations of parents and teachers. Student's belief that only perfectionism is acceptable. Star mentality. Emphasis on competition in the classroom.
Student shows a spark of life by trying to protect self from further hurt.	Student may want to succeed if he or she can be assured of not making mistakes and of achieving some status. For some severely discouraged students, there is no silver lining.
Build a caring relationship with the student. Teach student how to express hurt and hostility appropriately and invite student to talk to us when she or he is upset.	Encourage student to change self-perception from "I can't" to "I can." Help end student's social isolation by drawing the student into congenial relationships with us and other students.
Make a graceful exit. Use time-out. Set the consequences.	Modify instructional methods. Provide tutoring. Teach positive self-talk. Make mistakes okay. Build confidence. Focus on past success. Make learning tangible. Recognize achievement.

155

Teacher and Student Response Clues
to Identifying the Goal of Misbehavior

Teacher Response to Behavior

Behavior	Feelings	Action Impulse
Attention	Irritation Annoyance	Verbal
Power	Anger Frustration Fear	Physical
Revenge	Anger Frustration Fear Dislike Hurt Devastation	Fight or flight
Avoidance-of-Failure	Professional concern	Prescriptive or resigned to failure

Student Response to Intervention

Response Style	Response Action
Compliant	Stops misbehavior temporarily.
Confrontational	Misbehavior continues until stopped on student's terms.
Hurtful	Misbehavior continues and intensifies until stopped on student's terms.
Dependent	Continues to do nothing.

Summary Chart of Interventions

	General Strategy	*Techniques*
Attention-Seeking Behavior	Minimize the attention.	Ignore the behavior. Give "The Eye." Stand close by. Mention the student's name while teaching. Send a secret signal. Give written notice. Give an I-message.
	Legitimize the behavior.	Make a lesson out of the behavior. Extend the behavior to its most extreme form. Have the whole class join in the behavior. Use a diminishing quota.
	Do the unexpected.	Turn out the lights. Play a musical sound. Lower your voice. Change your voice. Talk to the wall. Use one-liners. Cease teaching temporarily.
	Distract the student.	Ask a direct question. Ask a favor. Change the activity.
	Notice appropriate behavior.	Thank students. Write well-behaved students' names on the chalkboard.
	Move the student.	Change the student's seat. Send the student to the thinking chair.

Power and Revenge Behaviors	Make a graceful exit.	Acknowledge students' power.
		Remove the audience.
		Table the matter.
		Make a date.
		Use a fogging technique:
		  Agree with the student.
		  Change the subject.

	Use time-out.	Time-out in the classroom. Time-out in another classroom. Time-out in a special room. Time-out in the office. Time-out in the home.

	General Strategy	Techniques
	Set the consequences.	Loss or delay of activity. Loss or delay of using objects or equipment. Loss or delay of access to school areas. Denied interactions with other students. Required interactions with school personnel. Required interactions with parents. Required interactions with police. Restitution: Repair of objects. Replacement of objects.
Avoidance-of-Failure Behavior	Modify instructional methods.	Use concrete learning materials and computer-assisted instruction. Teach one step at a time.
	Provide tutoring.	Extra help from teachers. Remediation programs. Adult volunteers. Peer tutoring. Learning centers.
	Teach positive self-talk.	Post positive classroom signs. Require two "put-ups" for every put-down. Encourage positive self-talk before beginning tasks.
	Make mistakes okay.	Talk about mistakes. Equate mistakes with effort. Minimize the effect of making mistakes.
	Build confidence.	Focus on improvement. Notice contributions. Build on strengths. Show faith in students. Acknowledge the difficulty of a task. Set time limits on tasks.
	Focus on past success.	Analyze past success. Repeat past success.
	Make learning tangible.	"I-Can" cans. Accomplishment Albums. Checklists of skills. Flowchart of concepts. Talks about yesterday, today, and tomorrow.
	Recognize achievement.	Applause. Clapping and standing ovations. Stars and stickers. Awards and assemblies. Exhibits. Positive time-out. Self-approval.

The Building Blocks of Self-Esteem

Helping Students Feel Capable

Make mistakes okay.
Talk about mistakes.
Equate mistakes with effort.
Minimize the effect of making mistakes.

Build confidence.
Focus on improvement.
Notice contributions.
Build on strengths.
Show faith in students.
Acknowledge the difficulty of a task.
Set time limits on tasks.

Focus on past success.
Analyze past success.
Repeat past success.

Make learning tangible.
"I-Can" cans.
Accomplishment Albums.
Checklists of skills.
Flowchart of concepts.
Talks about yesterday, today, and tomorrow.

Recognize achievement.
Applause.
Clapping and standing ovations.
Stars and stickers.
Awards and assemblies.
Exhibits.
Positive time-out.
Self-approval.

Helping Students Connect

Give students the five A's:
Acceptance.
Accept sincerely and unconditionally.
Accept students' personal style.

Attention.
Greet students.
Listen to students.
Teach students to ask for attention.
Spend time chatting.
Ask students about their life outside school.
Mention what you've talked about before.
Eat with students.
Invite students to eat in your room.
Attend school events.
Get involved in a project with students.
Schedule individual conferences.
Join students on the playground.
Chaperon school events.
Recognize birthdays.
Make baby-picture bulletin boards.
Send cards, messages, homework to absent students.
Show interest in students' work or hobbies.

Appreciation.
Describe the behavior accurately.
Use three-part appreciation statements.
Focus only on the present.
Give written words of appreciation.
Teach students to ask for appreciation.

Affirmation.
Be specific.
Be enthusiastic.
Acknowledge positive traits verbally or in writing.

Affection.
Show affection when things go badly.
Show kindness, and it will multiply and be returned.
Show friendship.
Use affectionate touch when appropriate.

Helping Students Contribute

Encourage students' contributions to the class.
Invite students' help with daily tasks.
Request students' curriculum choices.
Ask students' input for rules.

Encourage students to help other students.
Peer tutoring.
Peer counseling.
Peer recognition:
  Applause.
  Appreciation and affirmation statements.
  Happygrams.
  Appreciation password.

Cooperative Discipline School Action Plan

Name of student _____ Date _____

Step 1: Pinpoint and describe the child's behavior.	**Step 2: Identify the goal of the misbehavior.**	**Step 3: Choose intervention techniques.**

1. _____ _____ _____

   _____   _____

2. _____ _____ _____

   _____   _____

3. _____ _____ _____

   _____   _____

Step 4: Select encouragement techniques.

Capable: _____

_____

_____

Connect: _____

_____

_____

Contribute: _____

_____

_____

Continued on next page.

Step 5: Involve parents as partners.

1st phone call: Date _____   2nd phone call: Date _____

Parent Response: _____ Send School Action Plan   Parent response: _____

_____ Schedule conference   _____

Conference: Date _____   _____ Parent-teacher   _____ Parent-teacher-student

Others attending _____

Parent suggestions _____

_____

_____

Student suggestions _____

_____

_____

Suggestions of other participants _____

_____

_____

Home Action Plan developed? _____ Yes   _____ No

Follow-up conferences _____

_____

_____

_____

_____

APPENDIX F
Cooperative Discipline Home Action Plan

Name of child _____ Date _____

| **Step 1: Pinpoint and describe the child's behavior.** | **Step 2: Identify the goal of the misbehavior.** | **Step 3: Choose intervention techniques.** |

1. _____

_____

_____

2. _____

_____

_____

3. _____

_____

_____

Step 4: Select encouragement techniques.

Capable: _____

_____

_____

Connect: _____

_____

_____

Contribute: _____

_____

_____

APPENDIX G
Parent Resource Library

Albert, Linda. *Coping with Kids*. New York: Dutton, 1982; Ballantine, 1984.

———. *Coping with Kids and School*. New York: Dutton, 1984; Ballantine, 1985.

———. *Coping with Kids and Vacation*. New York: Ballantine, 1986.

Albert, Linda, and Michael Popkin. *Quality Parenting*. New York: Random House, 1987; Ballantine, 1989.

Berne, Patricia, and Louis Savary. *Building Self-Esteem in Children*. New York: Continuum, 1987.

Dinkmeyer, Don, et al. *The Effective Parent*. Circle Pines, Minn.: American Guidance Service, 1987.

Dinkmeyer, Don, and Gary D. McKay. *Padres Eficaces Con Entrenamiento Sistemático (PECES), Libro de los Padres*. Circle Pines, Minn.: American Guidance Service, 1981.

———. *Parenting Young Children: Helpful Strategies Based on Systematic Training for Effective Parenting (STEP) for Parents of Children Under Six*. Circle Pines, Minn.: American Guidance Service, 1989.

———. *Raising a Responsible Child*. New York: Simon & Schuster, 1973.

———. *Systematic Training for Effective Parenting (STEP), Parent's Handbook*. Circle Pines, Minn.: American Guidance Service, 1976.

———. *Systematic Training for Effective Parenting of Teens (STEP/Teen), Parent's Guide*. Circle Pines, Minn.: American Guidance Service, 1983.

Dreikurs, Rudolf, and Vicki Soltz. *Children: The Challenge*. New York: Dutton, 1964.

Einstein, Elizabeth, and Linda Albert. *Strengthening Your Stepfamily*. Circle Pines, Minn.: American Guidance Service, 1986.

Leman, Kevin. *Making Children Mind Without Losing Yours*. Old Tappan, N.J.: Fleming H. Revell, 1984.

Lott, Lynn, Riki Intner, and Marilyn Kientz. *Family Work: Whose Job Is It?* Santa Rosa, Calif.: Practical Press, 1988.

Main, Frank. *Perfect Parenting & Other Myths*. Minneapolis: CompCare Publications, 1986.

Nelsen, Jane. *Positive Discipline*. New York: Ballantine, 1987.

Slagle, Robert. *A Family Meeting Handbook: Achieving Family Harmony Happily*. Sebastopol, Calif.: Family Relations Foundation, 1985.

Albert, Linda, and Elizabeth Einstein. *Strengthening Stepfamilies*. Circle Pines, Minn.: American Guidance Service, 1986.

This program provides stepparents with the information necessary to understand their remarried family and the skills needed to improve troublesome situations. Stepfamily members learn how to communicate effectively, how to resolve conflicts, and how to structure their home life to improve relationships.

Dinkmeyer, Don, and Gary D. McKay. *Systematic Training for Effective Parenting (STEP)*. Circle Pines, Minn.: American Guidance Service, 1976.

STEP gives parents a practical and effective method for raising responsible, confident children. The program emphasizes respect and cooperation among all family members. Skills are taught through readings, recordings, discussions, and activities. Between sessions, parents apply what they've learned.

———. *Padres Eficaces Con Entrenamiento Sistemático (PECES)*. Circle Pines, Minn.: American Guidance Service, 1981.

This Spanish-language version of *STEP* will help Spanish-speaking parents improve their family relationships.

———. *Systematic Training for Effective Parenting of Teens (STEP/Teen)*. Circle Pines, Minn.: American Guidance Service, 1983.

STEP/Teen addresses the tough challenges of raising teens. It follows the same practical, workable principles that are offered in *STEP* and gives parents a way of opening communication during the years when it is most vital.

———. *Early Childhood STEP: Systematic Training for Effective Parenting (STEP) of Children Under Six*. Circle Pines, Minn.: American Guidance Service, 1989.

Adapts and expands the principles and techniques of *STEP* to the special challenges of parenting babies, toddlers, and preschoolers. Includes developmental information.

Dinkmeyer, Don, Sr., Gary D. McKay, Don Dinkmeyer, Jr., James S. Dinkmeyer, and Joyce L. McKay. *The Next STEP*. Circle Pines, Minn.: American Guidance Service, 1987.

This program helps parents practice and refine the skills they've learned in *STEP* and *STEP/Teen*. It introduces a new technique for helping parents—the problem-solving group. A companion video supplements the sessions.

Popkin, Michael H. *Active Parenting*. Atlanta: Active Parenting, Inc., 1982.

Active Parenting helps parents learn how to communicate effectively with their children, how to build mutual respect among family members, and how to discipline using natural and logical consequences.

———. *Active Parenting of Teens*. Atlanta: Active Parenting, Inc., 1989.

The *Active Parenting* program adapted to rearing teens.